WILDERNESS MOMENTS

WILDERNESS MOMENTS

How To Live Victoriously Through Them

JOSEPH B. ONYANGO OKELLO

Unless otherwise indicated, all passages of Scripture are derived from the New International Version of the Bible

ISBN-13: 9781533594228
ISBN-10: 1533594228

Dedicated to All Members of First United Methodist Church—Oviedo, FL

TABLE OF CONTENTS

Acknowledgements

I AM INDEBTED TO members of First United Methodist Church, Oviedo, (FUMCO) for their kindness and encouragement as they urged me to get this book published. Although my knowledge that our path would someday cross was not beyond the realm of possibility, the fact that those paths have crossed in this current way continues to strike me with a deeper sense of God's Providence—deeper than I previously had. I will remain forever grateful to God and to FUMCO for allowing me to serve you as your minister, though in a very small way.

I especially want to thank Debbie Burton who provided useful insights while editing the original manuscript, thereby saving me from making embarrassing errors. Her willingness to do this work is a great service to FUMCO and to the Lord Jesus Christ. I attribute all the clarity of expression to her. Of course, additional errors that might afflict this work are mine.

I also thank Charlene Davis for her invaluable counsel in helping me find a good publisher. The finance committee also offered great encouragement to me upon learning about my publishing intentions and the manner in which I intend to use possible proceeds arising from the sale of this work. I fully believe the cause is noble, and hopefully, it will help, in some way, to further God's work in many ways.

I also want to thank the faculty and staff of Asbury Theological Seminary, Dunnam Campus, for always making specific resources available for publishing works such as these. The library staff members, such as Father Michael Shaw and Wesley Custer, have always been available to point me to the right resources as I tried to put the thoughts of this work together.

I also thank my family, especially my wife whose patience continues to baffle me. Her willingness to allow me to spend numerous hours working on this manuscript as she battles cancer is a lesson worthy of mention. As I, together with our son Sean, anticipate her healing, she remained and continues to remain upbeat even in her current situation without losing her joy, during my absence from home, as I tried to beat important deadlines.

Finally, I wish to express my gratitude to God who truly walks with us every step of the way as we deal with wilderness moments. Without the assurance of his presence in our lives, those moments would afflict us with deep hopelessness. My family now knows, firsthand, what walking through the wilderness entails. I will no longer underestimate the excruciations members of my congregation go through as I hear them express the concerns they have about their afflictions. You are all in my prayers daily.

INTRODUCTION

LET ME INVITE you on a journey. It is a journey of reflection through the wilderness of life. I define this expression at the very first chapter of this work. A one-sentence definition may not exactly do justice to its understanding without an explication of the proper context. Therefore, I urge you to be patient with me as I postpone my definition of this work to that chapter.

For now, let me simply note to you that my family is currently walking through this wilderness. Once again, I will share more about this in the very first chapter of this work. What I want to note here is the fact that I do not believe we will be in the wilderness forever. I think in the end my family will walk out of this wilderness quite triumphantly, based not only on God's promises, but also on the testimony of those who have witnessed God walking with them through a similar journey.

Quite possibly, you too might be on this journey. To be sure, many individuals find themselves in this kind of wilderness. Therefore, you are in good company, though few travelers pause to reflect on its implications. I invite you to walk through this journey of reflection with me. I do not pretend to have all the answers. I know of no one who does, though I think you and I might find specific frameworks, through this reflection, that might enable us to live victoriously through those moments.

I have to admit that reflecting on these moments have been rather tough. I find myself dwelling more on the "what-if" aspect of the wilderness, namely, the unknown—along with its possible implication. Still, somewhere in the words of Scripture I find hope in the One who holds "what-if" instances in His hands. As you and I walk through the wilderness, the joy of reflecting on this journey reveals the truth that we are never alone. It reveals the truth that somewhere in the midst of the unknowns, God is walking with us as we take each step.

As you walk through this journey, it will involve tears coupled with laughter, sorrow coupled with joy, and sadness coupled with happiness. My goal in this work is to encourage you to find victory. One lesson I hope you will take from this reflection is the realization that even if God does not save us *from* the wilderness, he does intend to save us *through* the wilderness.

As Garth and Mervin Rosell note in their work *Shoe-Leather Faith*, God never promised to keep Job's afflictions from coming into Job's life. He never promised to keep Daniel from the lions' den. He never promised to keep the three Hebrew boys, Shadrack, Meshach and Abednego, from the fiery furnace. He did promise one thing, though: he promised he would be with them through their afflictions and to pull them through those afflictions victoriously.

The truth of that notion applies to you as well. God never promised to keep your wilderness moments from afflicting you. He never promised he would keep those trials and those challenges from knocking at your doorstep. But you can be sure of one promise God intends to keep: to be with you, even if you do not physically see or feel him, and to pull you through your afflictions victoriously.

I base these reflections on the wilderness of life on Deuteronomy 8:2–5 in order to underscore God's presence in one's life as one walks through the wilderness. For example, the first part of the book serves to underscore the importance of God allowing us to walk through the wilderness as a way, on God's part, of revealing to us the contents of our hearts— the stuff our hearts are made of. In other words, are we truly the kind of people we say we are in our relationship with the Lord? Only an experience in the wilderness of life can reveal this truth to us. The second part of the book tries to show, in various ways, the manner in which God humbles us. The third part of the book tries to underscore the lesson all of us ought to learn while walking through the wilderness, namely, learning to depend on God. The final part reminds us of the importance of allowing God to shape us. Having allowed the wilderness moment to reveal to us what is in our hearts, God gives us the opportunity to be shaped and disciplined in order to become more and more like him.

This summary lays out the general terrain of the book, and each chapter is short, designed to be read relatively quickly, giving the reader some time to pause for reflection before embarking on the next chapter. I hope you will find meaning and purpose, as I did, through your challenges as you struggle in this journey. I pray God will underscore his presence in your life as you read. Bon voyage.

Part One

Wilderness Moments

1

Their Nature

God has a specific salvific destiny for every human being—salvific because humans are fallen creatures in desperate need of redemption. Redemption, therefore, is our destiny, our promised land, so to speak. The apostle Paul reminds us of how God desires the salvation of all humans. This motif finds reiteration throughout the passages of Scripture. We all have a divinely designed destiny prepared for us. All we need in order to find ourselves on the path to this destiny is to express a willingness to embark on this journey.

However, a small—nay, a big—problem exists. I sum it up in one word: the wilderness. I refer, by this term, to experiences in life that seem to put your attainment of this destiny at risk. The examples abound in the spiritual world. Before pointing them out, let me illustrate one way in which they play themselves out. As I write these lines, I am sitting next to my wife at an infusion center 30 minutes from our home. Several weeks before this day, she was diagnosed with breast cancer. She is therefore undergoing chemotherapy in an effort to fight the cancer. Horror stories about the side effects of chemotherapy have been tossed our way. Meanwhile, friends from my church at First United Methodist Church of Oviedo were kind enough to babysit our five-year old son as I accompany my wife to the infusion center. The experience remains intensely difficult to countenance, both as a husband who always tries to fix broken things (I rarely succeed in this) and as a father who feels compelled to explain to his son what his mother is going through.

As I mentally rummage through these staggering realities, I have wondered, almost on an hour-by-hour-basis, why God would not directly heal my wife and save her from the gruesome side effects of chemotherapy. I have wondered why God would not immediately touch my wife with instantaneous healing to save me the agony of watching her contend with this situation. Surely, the path to direct instantaneous healing is much shorter, quicker, and more convenient. I have no easy answers to these questions. My assessment of the situation seems to revolve around the word I alluded to as the wilderness. We find ourselves currently in the wilderness contending with a situation bigger than ourselves. How God might be in the details draws me back to a fascinating experience detailed in the Old Testament.

I refer to how God delivered the children of Israel from bondage in Egypt. God had a specific salvific plan for them. Stated differently, he had a specific destiny for them—a destiny he personally described as a land flowing with milk and honey. Using Moses as his link person, God delivered the children of Israel from bondage. However, in order for them to arrive at their divinely designed destiny, they had to pass through the wilderness. Later in this work, I will revisit this very notion, and God's reasons for making them pass through the wilderness. All I urge you to bear in mind at this point is the importance of walking through the wilderness on the path to your salvific destiny.

This fact brings me back to my personal story. God seems to have a specific destiny for my family—a destiny he could quite easily accomplish through healing my wife directly. I have no doubt God has a good destiny for my family. I am more than convinced he could have used, if he wanted to, the shorter, more direct and quicker means of instantaneous healing and save my family the agony of living through an 18-week administration of chemotherapy. Seemingly God seems to be accomplishing this destiny through this wilderness of chemotherapy rather than through that shorter route of direct healing. After studying the Book of Exodus and the Book of Deuteronomy, I have begun wondering whether what played out corporately in the lives of the Israelites seems to be playing itself out, analogously, in my wife's life. Might she, might my family be finding itself walking through the wilderness, and if so, how, exactly, is this dynamic playing itself out?

Of course I am referring to the term wilderness in a very metaphorical sense. By that term I am not limiting it to its literal meaning. I also include, in that expression, the various undesirable and unpleasant experiences in life that test us, humble us, teach us and shape us. I know of no Christian who lives his or her life as a stranger to those experiences. They come in various packages—in moments of spiritual drought, in moments of physical pain, in moments of relational challenges, in moments of financial difficulties and sometimes, in death.

I call such moments "wilderness moments." Given the option, I would rather not experience them. To use the fairy tale expression, I would rather live happily ever after without going through a single second of wilderness moments. I want my life to be painless, to be stress free, to be comfortable, to be luxurious, and to be all rosy and plush. I do not wish to feel the crushing cruelty hitherto afforded by this universe. I know of no one who does.

To be sure, most of the institutions we put in place in this life seem, on the one hand, geared towards eliminating the wilderness moments we live through and, on the other, promoting our well-being. John Stuart Mill, the atheistic philosopher, seemed quite right in observing how pain and pleasure both function as our masters, and how we find ourselves enslaved by them,[1] though I think he was quite wrong in concluding, from that observation, that pain and pleasure function as the source and standard of our ethics. Just because wilderness moments punctuate the paths to our salvific destiny does not, thereby, imply our allegiance to them in terms of how to conduct our lives.

---

1 Mill, *On Liberty*

I have noted how such moments in the wilderness afflict our lives on the journey to our God-intended destiny. Let me, dispel a possible misconception that might arise from what I am trying to suggest here. I am not in any way trying to give reasons why I think God puts us through such moments. All I will be saying in these pages is fairly simple, namely: the path to our spiritual destiny is afflicted with wilderness moments, and when they do come our way, we should expect to be tested, we should expect to be humbled, we should expect to be taught, and we should also expect to be shaped, or for that matter, to be disciplined. The distinction, though quite a very thin one, must herein be made.

Quite likely, you the reader, can relate to those moments. You never planned to have them, but they came your way anyway. Strangely, good fortunes rarely come unless you somehow plan for them. Wilderness moments, however, come, and they do so even when we do not plan for them. The wilderness moments, though undesirable, somehow end up producing the best in us, specifically because, when we survive the tests, the humility, the lessons or the shaping brought about by those moments, we end up, in a certain sense, coming through them as better persons. They do have a positive side to them because they build our character in many important respects.

I bring these notions to your attention specifically because I suspect you, too, might be living through something similar. Quite possibly, you know someone living through such moments. What I will write about, then, in the next few chapters, could apply to you or someone you know, and you may find some valuable insights that could help you navigate through wilderness moments. Many believers in Christ go through these experiences. They seem to struggle with issues—issues they have prayed over for years and nothing seems to happen, and the feeling that God might have abandoned them becomes a reasonable explanation to them, though, of course, quite false, as we shall see later.

In my personal ministry, both in Africa and in the United States, I have met numerous individuals who, in my opinion, seemed to go through wilderness moments. They could see their lives falling apart right before their eyes, and they seemed unable to do anything about the situation. Hours of prayer and counsel seemed to yield little or no results. I met and talked to individuals whose spouses bailed out on them. The experience was extremely heart-rending in all ways for the abandoned spouse. The more we prayed and cried out to the Lord together, the more the abandoned spouse felt helpless and powerless throughout the entire experience.

One of the most difficult experiences was that of watching young children and their mother, preparing to bury their father, who died, in my opinion, a very premature death. Trying to come to terms with that experience was extremely difficult. No amount of explanation could answer the why-question raised by both the children and their mother throughout the ordeal. We mourned and cried with them. Besides the why-question, which they raised as many times as their energy could allow, they wondered why God seemed to have abandoned them in this way. This very question resurfaced quite frequently when counseling with individuals living through these wilderness moments.

An important aspect of wilderness moments I wish to highlight might be noted as follows. These moments do not come because those experiencing them have stopped believing in God. They still come in spite of sustained belief in God. The individuals seem to be quite happy with their faith. They seem to have their devotions regularly, praying and reading their Bibles without fail. They remained active in their churches, and remained extremely reliable and faithful when their churches counted upon them to execute specific responsibilities expected of them. In other words, they were not living through wilderness moments because they had backslidden. They lived through those moments in spite of remaining faithful to God and to the expression of their faith in God.

Has God abandoned such individuals? Is he done with them? Many people think so. To be sure, most thought patterns in the Western world find themselves tempted to arrive not merely at this conclusion, but to an even more radical conclusion, namely, that God does not exist. They believe that if God were the sort of Father Christians claim he is, or that if God really possesses the parental qualities often attributed to him by Christians, then he would not allow his children to suffer through those moments. For this reason, many in the Western world have yielded to the temptation of abandoning their faith. The gradual demise of Christianity in the United States, for example, is significant enough to allow scholars the liberty of classifying its spiritual status as post-Christian. Besides making unbelievable positive strides in technological advancements, and additional findings they classify as evidence for atheistic evolution, the reality of wilderness moments described in these pages continue to give the so-called free-thinking individuals the drive to wander away from Christianity.

How should we respond to the challenge presented by wilderness moments? What sort of advice should we give, if any, when countenancing individuals struggling with these moments? Does the Bible, whose credibility victims of wilderness moments seem to begin to question, offer any defense for itself? We will try to answer these questions, in this book, as we try to navigate through this difficult subject. Easy answers remain unavailable. However, by this fact I do not say that *any* answers are unavailable at all. They are available, but extremely difficult to embrace. Therefore, the honest soul-searching believer must contend and wrestle with the difficult answers given to the issues presented by these moments. Let us see if we can tackle the difficulties presented by this problem in the next section.

2

THE SPIRITUAL DIFFICULTY OF THE ISSUE

I HAVE ALREADY ALLUDED to the difficulty presented by this issue when I made reference to its effect on the Western world. Let me give it a slightly more extended treatment here. What I find fascinating, when comparing the Western mind's response to this issue with the African mind, is this: the Western mind seems ready to abandon belief in God when that belief becomes difficult, especially when God does not seem to come through in such moments.

New Testament scholars such as Bert Ehrman, for example, remain unafraid to abandon belief in God specifically because if God is who Christians claim he is then he should rescue them from suffering. Bear in mind that Professor Ehrman started off as an evangelical Christian, studied at an evangelical institution, and continued in his faith in God until he started teaching in college. While teaching a certain aspect of this very subject, he found that the implications of human suffering troubled him deeply, to a point of changing his mind about his long-held belief in the existence of God.[2] Thankfully, the struggles depicted by Professor Ehrman have been adequately and brilliantly answered by notable scholars such as Alvin Plantinga, former chair of the Department of Philosophy at the University of Notre Dame. Trying to show how Professor Plantinga formulated his answer to the sorts of challenge professor Ehrman raised will take us off topic.[3] For this reason, I will focus on how this issue affects the African mind.

Many African believers, by contrast, seem hesitant to jump to the conclusion that God does not exist by merely looking at the facts of suffering, or in our case, by experiencing wilderness moments. What they seem ready to countenance seems to be the possibility that God might not, after all, be trusted to walk with them through their trials. They understand the fact that God is a spiritual being, and they know that spiritual beings often remain visually inaccessible. For this reason, the idea of God's absence in times of suffering remains a reasonable conclusion. Just the same, God's absence does not imply, for the believing African, God's nonexistence. What it seems to imply is the notion of abandonment. The African believer, therefore, who struggles through the reality of wilderness moments might conclude, and quite possibly even feel, that God has abandoned him or her.

The problem can be stated briefly as follows. If God is truly the powerful parental figure portrayed in the Bible and

---

2 Erhman,

3 See the Appendix for a brief outline of the debate

preached about in churches, then surely he must be willing and able to rescue his children from the miseries brought about during their wilderness moments, for that is what thoughtful parents do when their children suffer. The reality depicts an absentee God who does not seem to rescue his children from suffering. God, therefore, is perhaps not the parental figure portrayed in the Bible and preached about in churches. If he is not the parental figure of this sort, then he could, quite plausibly, abandon his children when they suffer. For this reason, the claim that God will rescue his children from suffering seems doubtful.

Several pastoral responses could be given to this mindset, some of them adequate, and some, quite possibly inadequate. For the sake of brevity, let me focus on the responses, I believe, seem adequate. First, the fact that God *seems* distant does not necessarily imply that God *is* distant. God's invisible presence is a very real possibility. Moreover, in his invisible presence during those moments, he may quite conceivably be walking with the suffering believer in a way that underscores his divine support rather than withdrawal of his support. To be sure, he may not be answering the believers' prayers in the manner expected of him by the believer. For his own divine reasons, he may suspend immediate answers to prayer possibly with the goal of accomplishing bigger redemptive purposes as in the case of Job. I intend to provide an extended treatment of these purposes in later sections in this book. The main idea to underscore here is the Biblical fact that God's *apparent* distance does not imply God's *actual* distance. His invisible presence is a Biblical reality.

If you are not interested in philosophical reasoning, I suggest you skip this paragraph and proceed to the next one, which outlines the second response to the mindset alluded to earlier. The line of thought continues without missing much of the argument. For those interested in philosophical reasoning, this paragraph tries to show how God's apparent absence does not necessarily mean he is actually absent. The argument runs as follows: in order for our ever-present (or omnipresent) God to live inside his children and as close to all of his children as he promised, he would have to exist in the realm of the immaterial spiritual world. If he chose to do so in a material form of existence, his existence everywhere, including inside his children would not only be a clumsy interaction wherein we would be bumping into him at every juncture, it would also imply completely displacing us from our specific locations. Think about it in this way: if God is everywhere as we Christians believe, then he occupies every space. However, if he must occupy every space existing today, he must exist in an immaterial entity for at least one reason: if we insisted that our omnipresent God should show up in his full omnipresent material reality, his omnipresence would completely dislocate us from our various locations into oblivion. Thus for God to remain omnipresent, he must exist as an immaterial spiritual entity. If he exists as an immaterial spiritual entity, he would be invisible to the naked eye. This fact alone explains why God can be understood to be close to you and me, yet unseen. This fact further means that just because God seems apparently absent does not mean he is physically absent.

Second, just because God has not acted in our timeline does not mean he is not acting in his timeline. God's time-line remains quite different and superior to our timeline. This truth gets powerfully illustrated in the life of King Saul.[4] He found himself in danger of attack from the Philistines, and he knew he could not go to war before offering some kind of sacrifice to God. However, he was not authorized to offer the sacrifice. He had to wait for the prophet of God, Samuel, to offer the sacrifice. In Saul's timeline, prophet Samuel was delaying and Israel was getting dangerously close to going to war. Therefore, Saul decided to offer the sacrifice, only to have Samuel show up immediately after he offered the sac-rifice. Specifically because of this act of disobedience, God rejected Saul as King. The immediate lesson here, of course, is simple: wait on God, however long the waiting seems to be. God's timeline is not our timeline, and we must trust him to do what he, in his sovereignty sees as the overall picture. What we see is a very minute fraction of the overall scheme of things. For this reason, we are not equipped to say adequately that God was late in acting.

One more illustration of how God's timeline differs from ours finds expression in the death of Lazarus.[5] Bear in mind that Jesus knew how sick Lazarus was. In spite of this knowl-edge he waited until Lazarus was dead for four days. From a human perspective, death remains irredeemable, and worse if one is dead for four days. Lazarus' sisters, from their own

---

4 See 1 Samuel 13
5 See John 11

perspective, believed Jesus was too late to do anything for Lazarus. If we ever had a classic illustration of a wilderness moment, the story of Lazarus gives it one of the best expressions. The sisters felt abandoned by Christ, and they never hesitated to express their feelings immediately when Christ showed up. They knew the situation could not be redeemed and, again, they made this known to their Lord. Quite fascinatingly, what moved Jesus, was neither the fact that he was absent during Lazarus' illness nor the fact that he showed up "too late to do anything." What moved Jesus was the emotional pain resulting from the death of Lazarus.

These two observations provide at least two lessons for us, one of which we have already seen, namely: God's timeline is quite different from our timeline. Just because God appears late on our timeline does not mean that God is actually late. God can raise a person dead for four days and still be on time to save the person from illness! The second lesson can be captured as follows: the fact that Jesus wept and also was deeply moved by the death of Lazarus implies that God does not remain indifferent to our wilderness moments. They trouble him more than they trouble us because they trouble him at the eternal realm with an internally deeper intensity. For this reason, the notion that God lacks compassion for his struggling children who might be living through wilderness moments remains a non-starter in the Biblical world.

Therefore, besides the struggles of pain and suffering, the spiritual difficulty raised by wilderness moments is the notion of abandonment by God and the subsequent loneliness that follows from this abandonment, as exemplified by

Saul, and to a more intense extent, by the life of Lazarus. This difficulty is the sort of difficulty which needs to be addressed. How, for example, can the believer in the wilderness be assured that God has not abandoned him or her? The story of Lazarus gives us a clue. Even when God seems distant, as Jesus was when he first received the news that Lazarus was ill, God actually is near. How else would Jesus have known that Lazarus was sick if he was not, in some way, in close proximity to Lazarus? This provides us with the assurance that you and I can trust in God's nearness during wilderness moments.

3

WHY DO WE HAVE WILDERNESS MOMENTS?

WHY WE HAVE wilderness moments is a question whose answer remains elusive both to the scholar and the pastor alike. I do not pretend to have answers deeper than those already provided in both the scholarly and pastoral worlds. What I plan to do here is to re-sensitize believers to possible answers already available. I begin by noting, for example, that the Christian believer knows how the genesis of wilderness moments can be traced back to the spiritual world, though he or she may not be able to explain fully the exact details of how they begin to play themselves out. Something cognitively inaccessible to us seems to be going on there. We do know from Scripture, for example, why Job was afflicted. Owing to his deep devotion to God, the enemy's purpose was to get Job to curse God. One must bear in mind that cursing God in the Old Testament world was blasphemy, an offense punishable by death.[6] It was an expression of outright rebellion against God. In a certain sense, it was the ultimate sin. The goal of getting Job to commit this ultimate sin lay at the heart of the enemy's intentions for Job.

Therefore, the enemy did everything he could to get Job to curse God. He began with Job's wealth and destroyed everything Job owned. He wanted to see if Job would curse God the moment he lost all his wealth. Of course Job's faithfulness remained intact. Having failed in this, the enemy tried to get Job to curse God by destroying Job's children. Once again, Job's faith remained intact and he never cursed his Lord. The third attack came when the enemy attacked Job's health. Still, Job clung to his faith with remarkable tenacity. The final attack from the enemy was launched against Job—and by extension, against God—through the words of Job's wife when she urged him to curse God and die. Seemingly, the attack was a final desperate attempt on the part of the enemy to get Job to curse God. Once again, Job's faith remained intact.

I noted, earlier, that we do know why the enemy afflicted Job, and I think we have seen why. We must now ask: do we know why God allowed the enemy to afflict Job? The answer seems readily available. However, perhaps that answer might be quite difficult for some believers to accept. Remember, God had reminded the enemy of Job's impeccable faith in God. The enemy challenged God's confidence in Job's faith. The reason God allowed the attack on Job was, therefore,

---

6 See Leviticus 24:15-16

to prove to the enemy that God was not mistaken about his confidence in Job's faith, even though God was, clearly, not happy that his confidence in Job's faith had to be proven in this painful way to the enemy.

The reason some believers might find this explanation difficult finds its basis on the following question: surely God could have chosen a better method to prove to the enemy that Job's faith was intact. God could have, for example, chosen a non-painful method of accomplishing this task. Note, however, that a non-painful method, in a world such as ours, would quite possibly not have convinced the enemy. Remember, in this case, the enemy believed that pain was the enemy's best way to get job to curse God. In short, God turned the enemy's standards, of achieving unbelief, on its own head in order to show the enemy how mistaken he was in believing he could get Job to curse his God.

We get a snippet of a similar scenario playing itself out in the life of Peter, the disciple of Jesus. One will recall how Jesus told Peter that the enemy had asked for permission to "sift Peter as wheat." Interestingly, Jesus reminded Peter that he had prayed for Peter in order for Peter's faith to remain intact. As we well know, Peter, denied three times that he knew his Lord—a stark contrast from Job's response who, in the midst of severe affliction, remained completely committed to God. After he rose from the dead, Jesus re-instated Peter, asking Peter to take care of Christ's sheep.

From both instances, the wilderness moments created by the enemy seem to have the intention of getting faithful believers to abandon their faith. Quite fascinatingly, this goal seems to get fulfilled in the Western world, where the reality of pain and suffering leaves them to conclude, logically, that belief in God must be abandoned. Might one be right in thinking that the enemy is registering some successes in these areas?

So far I have looked at the wilderness moments created by the enemy, and I have shown how these moments have the intention of causing believers to turn away from God, or to rebel against God. What would we say about the wilderness moments created by God? Pieces of evidence for such moments, seemingly, appear in several portions of Scripture. My purpose in this book is to dwell on such moments and determine their implications for our lives should we find ourselves countenancing them. When God causes his children to live through wilderness moments, the aim would not be of the sort brought about by the enemy. The goal of the enemy is to cause believers to abandon belief in God, or bring the believers to a point of rebellion against God. The goal God has in mind seems different, however, and I try to outline them in subsequent sections of this book. Before I embark on this feature, notice how such moments find expression quite forcefully in certain portions of Scripture where God himself declares his intentions for his children whenever they live through these moments. Seemingly, God tries to accomplish certain purposes in his goals and intentions. Those purposes seem to have spiritual maturity as their goal, trying to make believers more and more like Christ, reflecting the glory of his image in specific junctions of their lives.

As I alluded to in the previous chapter, a good example of such moments can be found in the book of Deuteronomy 8:1–5. In that portion of Scripture, Moses addresses the children of Israel, giving them reasons why God brought the Israelites through the desert. In other words, Moses is allowing the children of Israel to see that their 40-year journey through the wilderness was not a machination of the enemy. It was the purpose of God, and that God had a four-fold goal he intended to accomplish in the lives of his children. This fact underscores the observation concerning some wilderness moments, namely, they are, indeed, caused by God, and that he brings about specific purposes in allowing those moments to come our way.

Whereas we can see from Scripture that God seems to be the cause of such moments, the believer must be left wondering how, when wilderness moments come, to distinguish between those caused by God and those caused by the enemy. I will offer a fuller explanation of this reason when I draw your attention to why God chose the longer route through the wilderness rather than the shorter route. For now, let me admit how this question seems fair. Remember, according to our findings from Scripture, those caused by the enemy seem aimed at leading us to abandon our faith in God. Those caused by God seem aimed at leading us to greater heights of spiritual maturity. Where, then, does one draw the distinction between the kinds of wilderness moments caused by the enemy and the one caused by God?

The answer to this question is not an easy one to find, and this takes me back to a comment I made earlier: something cognitively inaccessible to us seems to be going on here whenever we countenance such moments. Stated differently, whatever goes on at the spiritual world that brings about those moments, we really do not know them. However, we still can know one important thing, which, I think, helps us to deal with such difficulties. However, providing this explanation will take some space.

First, take the life of Job, as an example. Job knew how, in spite of his afflictions, he would experience some level of spiritual maturity. Notice his words when he says, "When he tests me I will come forth as gold."[7] He knew how in spite of his unjustified suffering, he would still experience the benefit of spiritual maturity way beyond the kind of maturity he would have acquired had he not suffered as much. Second, he experienced God's presence in a way he would not have experienced before when God finally showed up to answer some of the questions he raised as he suffered. In other words, God showed up to prove to Job that Job had not been abandoned. Moreover, and this counts as the third issue, Job learned additional lessons, acquired from reflecting on the numerous questions God asked him even as he suffered.

I point these facts out to note that the believer can still benefit from wilderness moments launched against him or her by the enemy in the following way: God can turn those moments into moments of spiritual maturity. Stated differently, even when the enemy uses those moments to cause believers to turn away from God, God himself turns those

7 Job 23:10

moments into opportunities for the believers' spiritual growth. This fact seems to be the case for every believer experiencing wilderness moments. This fact, of course, implies that whereas the question of the origin of the wilderness moments is, indeed, an important one, believers know that God can use wilderness moments to make them more mature in him. The enemy used wilderness moments to turn Job away from God. God, however, used those very moments not only to turn Job into an even more faithful follower of God, but also to prove to the enemy (in quite a humiliating way) that he was profoundly wrong about Job's faithfulness and character.

4

The Tentative Implications

Before launching deeper into the aspects of maturity
we find when living through wilderness moments, let
me state some preliminary implications for individuals finding themselves in this uncomfortable situation. First, even
though the cause and origin of our wilderness moment is,
most certainly, a very important thing to want to know (i.e.
whether or not their origin can be traced back to God or
to the enemy), we can rest assured that God can turn those
unfortunate moments into opportunities for our spiritual
growth.

A blind acquaintance reminded me of the benefits he has,
hitherto, gained from his blindness, namely, that he finds
himself completely shielded from lust of the eyes. He knows
he is no longer vulnerable to this kind of lust because he has
nothing to see. Whereas, admittedly, his blindness continues
to be an unfortunate thing, he remains thankful he has, at

least, one major aspect of sin he no longer has cause to worry about. For him, it remains a non-issue.

Another friend, whose daughter received a severe affliction from a mosquito bite while swimming in a pond in one of the cities in Florida, watched his daughter's health deteriorate to the point of death. For several years the child lived almost in a coma. Watching one's child deteriorate before one's eyes in this way must be one of the most heart-rending things a parent could endure. What I found almost incomprehensible was my friend's view of the whole scenario as it played itself out before his eyes year after year. He would remind me that because of his child, God had opened up for him numerous possibilities he found extremely difficult to trade for anything else. In his view, whether the enemy caused the mosquito to bite his child or something else mattered very little. What mattered to this friend were the personal levels of maturity both he and his wife attained when they sensed God's deep presence in their lives while experiencing these difficult circumstances.

In reminiscing over this fact, an even closer friend had what, at that time, was the unfortunate experience of bringing into this world a child with Down's Syndrome. The troubling issue was the fact that throughout their pregnancy, the condition remained undetected by the doctors. Imagine their consternation when, immediately after delivery, the symptoms of Down Syndrome showed up when the mother held her baby in her arms. That reality was a fact too difficult to accept for the parents, and, of course, for us. However, over the years, this child has grown to be the sweetest little girl they could ever have, and the parents express their delight on a daily basis that this little girl came their way.

Numerous other stories illustrate the point for believers, namely: irrespective of the origin of one's wilderness moments, God can still turn those moments around, and bring the best out of the victim's lives in very unprecedented ways. We know this fact to hold for us as believers because numerous pieces of evidence abound in our lives to assure us of this fact.

However, we must ask: in what ways, exactly, should we see God as bringing out the best in us when we live through these moments? How exactly is he doing it? In order to answer this question, I turn to the very passage alluded to earlier, namely: Deuteronomy 8:1–5. This passage gives us a snapshot of what God might be trying to accomplish in the lives of his children when he allows wilderness moments to come their way. To be sure, the passage seems to apply even to cases caused by the enemy himself, even though not explicitly stated. I make this contention because each ingredient mentioned in this passage of the purposes of wilderness moments finds full illustration in Job's life in a very fascinating way, and because I promised earlier to address this issue when treating the reasons God presented, in the book of Exodus, for having Israel take longer route through the wilderness, I now address it below.

A fascinating fact we find in Israel's redemption seems to be the length of time God took to accomplish the purposes he intended for them. Consider, for example, that the children of Israel would have taken a significantly shorter time than the length of time they actually took to reach the Promised Land.

Scholars remind us that had the children of Israel taken the shorter route to the Promised Land, they would have taken about eight days to reach their destination. Following that route seemed the logical thing to do.

Interestingly, God decided to take them through the much longer route of having to cross the desert. God's reason was very simple. He knew that if he took them through the shorter route, they would encounter violent military opposition from enemies unknown to them, and then they would abandon their pursuit of redemption into the Promised Land.[8] For this reason, God chose to take them through a route that took them 40 years rather than eight days.

The tentative preliminary lesson here, of course, seems obvious and that lesson seems applicable not only to my wife's battle with cancer, which I alluded to in an earlier chapter, but quite possibly, to your situation as well. Sometimes what appears to be the logical solution to our problems, from our perspective may not necessarily be the right perspective. In some ways it might be the disastrous perspective. I have often wondered whether some goals in our lives as a family could not be accomplished except by walking through the wilderness of cancer—goals whose absence would have left us spiritually more bankrupt than we already are. Notice how, for the children of Israel, the logical solution would be to follow the shortest and fastest route to the Promised Land of well-being. However, God pointed out that they would have been discouraged by the violence that would have erupted. They

---

8 See Exodus 13:22

needed to be introduced to that kind of lifestyle in portions and not in one full blown out experience.

Similarly for us, we have many logical solutions to our problems. Unfortunately, those solutions may not necessarily be the right solutions, and often, in our attempt to be logical in solving those problems we end up finding ourselves in deeper problems. As a philosopher, I can vouch for the reality that just because something strikes us as logical does not mean it entails moral rightness. The proper solutions may take time, and will require great patience on our part to allow God to accomplish his goals for us. In all these, God wants us and expects us to trust in him and in his guidance specifically because he eternally remains in possession of the bigger picture. He has access to the various solutions to all our problems and difficulties.

Besides individuals such as Jesus' friend Lazarus, and the Apostle Paul, we find additional characters whose lives seemed to reflect this very motif. Consider, for example, the case of Joseph, Jacob's son. One will recall how God seemed to reveal to Joseph, through dreams on two different occasions, that he would be a highly respected government official. In one of the dreams Joseph dreamt he was in the fields collecting ears of corn. As he carried on with this activity, 11 ears of corn bowed to his ear of corn. Immediately upon relaying that dream to his family, Joseph's brothers understood the dream to mean he would one day rule over them, and they took offense at Joseph. On a second occasion, Joseph dreamed he saw 11 stars, including the sun and the moon, all bowing down before his star. Once again, Joseph's brothers, and Jacob his father, understood the meaning of the dream, and apparently, seemed to take offense at its implications—for this time the dream did not merely imply that only Joseph's brothers would be ruled by Joseph; it also implied the rule would be extended to Joseph.

Here, then, is the logical concern from a human standpoint. If this dream was really from God (and we know it was), logic seemed to suggest that God would whisk Joseph in some direct way from his home to the position of leadership he had for Joseph. One would expect, for example, that Joseph would meet up with someone from Egypt who would seem quite impressed with Joseph's skills and offer him a job, which would eventually have him promoted to that position of leadership.

Strangely, God chooses a different route. Joseph, upon request from his father, takes food to his brothers. However, rather than welcome Joseph as their brother, they conspire to kill him. After some kind of self-reflection, the brothers change their mind about killing Joseph—their own flesh and blood. Instead they throw him into a pit and, later, sell him, as a slave, to some Ishmaelites, who, in turn, sell him to Potiphar. While at Potiphar's house, Potiphar's wife falsely accuses Joseph of sexual misconduct, and Potiphar throws him in jail. The Bible then makes a comment worth remembering— even in jail, God was with Joseph.

However, while in jail, things were not as logical as one would have expected them to be. Two of Pharaoh's employees, a cupbearer and a baker, were there in jail, and both had dreams whose meaning remained elusive to them. Joseph interprets their dreams with 100 percent accuracy. Three days later, Pharaoh restores his chief cupbearer to his original position in complete fulfillment of Joseph's prediction. Pharaoh's baker, however, was not lucky. He was hanged just as Joseph had predicted. All events happened according to Joseph's interpretation of the dreams. Joseph then asks the cupbearer to remember him in his newly restored service to Pharaoh. One would imagine that God would use this experience immediately to Joseph's benefit. Besides being sold as a slave and being wrongfully accused of sexual misconduct, Joseph remains in jail for two more years. Only after those two years were over do we find the cupbearer remembering his sin of forgetfulness. After Pharaoh had a nightmare that needed interpretation, the cupbearer was then able to remember countenancing Joseph, the very person who accurately predicted his restoration to Pharaoh's service. Only then was Joseph able to get out of jail and be brought before Pharaoh to interpret Pharaoh's dream. Obviously, this experience was a long wait for Joseph to see his dream realized.

Notice, however, that Joseph, at no time, lost his faith in God. He remained faithful to the end even when he seemed to have every reason to turn away from God. Once again, consider the two possibilities. The first one of directly bringing Joseph to Pharaoh's service as second only to Pharaoh in command without having to subject Joseph to slavery and to false accusations. The other possibility is of indirectly bringing Joseph to this very destiny, by allowing him to be sold into slavery and to be accused of attempted rape, and then thrown in jail.

Through these experiences, not only do we see the nature and content of the heart of Joseph's brothers, but also the maturity Joseph displayed in terms of character. Not only do we see the humbling experience the brothers went through when they realized that the person they despised was made King through God's divine providence, we also see Joseph's humble spirit of willingness to forgive his brothers even when he had every reason to pay back. Not only do we see how Joseph learned to depend on God every step of the way, we also see how the brothers learned the seriousness of their mistake when they began confessing their errors while begging Joseph for leniency. Even more importantly, the experience shaped and disciplined Joseph's brothers in profound ways. Their lies were exposed to their father, and they, once again, found themselves pleading for forgiveness. Would Joseph and his brothers have realized or attained these states of affairs without Joseph's wilderness moments? Whereas answering in the negative might come across as needlessly dogmatic, skepticism about an affirmative answer to the question ought to strike us as rather unrealistic.

Joseph is not the only Old Testament character that lived through the wilderness. Abraham had his own experiences as well. Recall how both he and his wife Sarah longed to have children. For decades they remained barren. God, however, promised Abraham that he would be the father of many nations. Clearly, that promise would not be possible if Abraham was barren and if both of them were well advanced in years. Against all odds, God enabled them to have Isaac.

More surprising, however, was the command God gave Abraham to offer Isaac as a sacrifice to God. If God was promising to give Abraham the fatherhood of many nations, circumventing that promise by requiring Abraham to offer Isaac as a sacrifice was clearly not a logical way of achieving this goal. From their barrenness up to the time of offering Isaac as a sacrifice, we see Abraham and Sarah finding themselves in a wilderness of sorts.

The story of David is another example of an Old Testament character experiencing a wilderness moment. Recall how Samuel anointed David King of Israel. One would have expected David to live quite peacefully with Saul until David's time to become king had arrived. Unfortunately, the story did not turn out in this way. Saul became jealous of David, and tried to take David's life. Consequently, David found himself running for his life for decades. While running away from Saul, David wrote some of the most powerful portions of Scripture we all use for our spiritual nourishment. He was literally in the wilderness before he finally became King of Israel.

Why would God not just do things directly? Why does he have to take them through wilderness experiences? The answers to these questions may not be exactly clear. However, when we read the passage in Deuteronomy 2:1–8, it seems to suggest a four-fold purpose of wilderness moments. First of all, according to Moses' homily to the children of Israel, he seems to suggest that the Israelite's wilderness moment was for the purpose of testing them in order to see what was in their hearts. Second, God had the goal of humbling the Israelites. Third, God wanted to teach the Israelites to depend on him. Finally, God's intention was to discipline the

Israelites. Earlier in this first part of the book I promised to give an extended treatment of the purposes God might have in allowing wilderness moments to come our way. In what follows, I intend to honor this promise by giving these four-fold goals an extended treatment.

PART TWO

THE TEST

5

THE NEED FOR TESTS

I SPENT THE FIRST part of this book discussing the nature of wilderness moments. In this, and subsequent parts of this book, I intend to focus on what these moments bring out in our lives. Whereas what they bring out may not necessarily be their intended goals, they seem to produce certain desirable by-products. These by-products seem to be of the sort we would not have received under different circumstances, and they seem, in turn, to be for our own good.

When we read Deuteronomy 8:1–5, the first thing wilderness moments accomplish in our lives is the idea of testing those among us living through those very moments. Consider what verse two says: "Remember how the Lord your God led you all the way in the desert these 40 years, to humble you and to test you in order to know what was in your heart." In other words, those wilderness moments seem to come to us as some kind of hurdle we must jump, or some bridge we must cross. Importantly, however, they come to us as tests.

When I was in school, whether primary school, high school, or college, I had a morbid fear of tests. The final exams terrified me immensely. The situation did not seem to improve when I enrolled in graduate and post-graduate school. Of course I understood what the tests tried to accomplish. Just the same, I wondered how life would appear to me without the hassle of sitting down to study for the exam and then taking it.

I well recall how I prepared for my post-graduate exam, and how, in my first and second attempts, I did not get a passing grade. Both instances of failure traumatized me. Preparing for the third attempt at taking the exam was exhausting. Imagine the joy I got when my examiner called me, screaming through the phone speakers and delightedly announcing I had passed the exam. That message was great news to me. At that time I began to appreciate the fact that I had been tested and declared fit for the program in which I was enrolled. I was glad the entire ordeal was behind me. Before the exam, I disliked the rigor involved in preparing for it. After the exam I appreciated the fact of living through that experience.

A colleague of mine at my workplace once told me how he enjoyed preparing to run marathons. However, his preparation to run a half marathon with his wife was anything but pleasant. For some reason, neither he nor his wife enjoyed the many miles they had to cover in preparation to run the half-marathon, and this fact was surprising specifically because he had run full marathons before. Logically speaking, running half marathons would be relatively easier. They finally ran and completed the half marathon. Strangely, though, both were delighted the marathon was over, and my colleague seemed ready to run additional marathons.

Intentionally or not, preparing to accomplish as difficult a feat as running a marathon, or to study for an important exam, seems an extremely unpleasant thing. One might actually refer to it as a wilderness moment. However, it seems to prepare one for the kind of test in a way that brings out in us what would, under normal circumstances, not come out. This fact seems quite illustrative of the by-product of testing us yielded by wilderness moments.

Consider, also, how car manufacturers subject their new products to crash tests. The aim of such tests it to give them an idea of the survival rates of potential passengers should the car in question get involved in an accident. Ordinarily, cars that fail the crash tests remain unreleased into the market until the manufacturers make relevant adjustments enabling the cars to fare better in future tests.

Certain piano manufacturers also make their products following this principle of endurance. The pieces of wood used for manufacturing pianos get selected from trees known for withstanding some of the most violent storms and winds. Piano manufacturers interested in building pianos whose wood could withstand the tightest possible tensile pull from piano strings, ordinarily, locate trees growing in zones known for strong winds and violent storms. They know how the finest music can only be produced from materials known for weathering the toughest storms. Of course, the manufacturers would, therefore, not go for any piece of wood available at the market. Only the strongest pieces of wood will do—of the sort that nature 'seems to prepare' for this very task.

In a book entitled *A Man Called Peter*, Peter's wife tells the story of how her husband, who was a minister, paid specific attention to detail at almost every aspect of his life. He would not settle for mediocre stuff, whether it entailed preaching a sermon, or buying pieces of furniture. Whenever he went to a furniture store to buy, say, a wooden chair or stool, he always tested the strength of whatever items he bought. Assuming, for example, the shopkeeper assured him that the stool he wanted to buy was strong, Peter would take a few steps back, run towards the chair, jump as high as he could and then sit on the chair on his way down. His goal was to see if the chair was as sturdy as the shopkeeper braggedturdy enough to withstand the force of his entire body landing on it. Several chairs broke in the process, much to the consternation of the shopkeeper. Those that survived earned his endearment. Peter knew that a good chair happens to be the kind of chair able to take the heaviest human weight.[9]

I use all these stories to illustrate an important aspect of our lives. Deeply ingrained in our being is the belief that a thing is not worth having if it fails a certain test. A car is not worth buying if it fails a crash test. A piano will not produce good music if its frames comprise of weak planks of wood. A chair will not fulfill its purpose of being a chair if it buckles

---

9 *A Man Called Peter*

under ordinary weight. We consider these ordinary illustrations commonsensical. We should, therefore, and by analogy, find it commonsensical that certain tests in life may be required and expected of us. The nature of those tests varies from person to person depending on each person's level of maturity. Nonetheless, they seem quite necessary for specific reasons, some of which I will detail in the next section.

6

A Personal Experience of the Test

Without a doubt, wilderness moments, of the kind I have alluded to in the first part of this book, tend to put our faith to the test. Some of those tests can be fairly mild. Others, however, tend to be extremely severe. I recall a mild test when I was asked to speak in chapel in one of the universities in Kenya. Dutifully, I prepared, both in spirit and in research, for the speaking engagement, and put together what I thought was a fairly preachable sermon, though, of course, I approached that engagement, as I do with other speaking engagement with fear and trembling. I simply expounded on the passage from 1 Timothy 4:12, where Paul urged Timothy not to let those over whom he ministered look down on him because he was a young pastor. Instead, Paul urged and Timothy was to set an example to all believers in speech, in life, in love, in faith and in purity.

My intention, at that time, was to encourage the college students to set a good example to the rest of the world specifically because someone was, quite possibly, learning from their example secretly. That learner would then acquire pointers on how he or she would navigate through analogous issues in life. After completing my sermon, I believed I had driven the point home quite well, and, in a certain sense, was pleased to see how the sermon was so well received.

I did not know, however, that soon I would fail the very test I urged my listeners to pass. I intended to travel by bus from one city to the next, and that experience required going to the bus-station and buying a ticket for my travel. When I reached the bus station, I was delighted to discover that a good seat in the bus was available for me. To be sure, it was a prized seat—the kind of seat given on a first-come first-served basis. I could not believe my ears when I was told I could have the seat, and it came to me at the price of other regular seats. I was assured the bus would get to my intended destination at a certain time, and this arrival would give me just enough time to attend a choir meeting later that evening.

However, a certain peculiarity with a majority of the Kenyan system of transportation is that for most buses, travel only begins when the buses are full rather than when the clock strikes a certain hour. For this reason, we still had to wait for the bus to fill up before we could take off, and that is where my problems slowly began. Shortly before the bus finally filled up with passengers, the bus company's CEO, for some reason, needed to travel to the same destination as mine. Unfortunately, he was not planning to use his car. He chose to travel by bus—more specifically, by the bus I had booked; and because he was the CEO, my seat was taken away from me and was given to him.

When this happened, I lost my composure. The folks who came to me to ask me to yield my seat to the company's CEO happened to be at the receiving end of my verbal protest. I was extremely vocal about this unfair change of seats on my part. I refused to compromise. I insisted on my rights. I made sure the CEO knew that I cared very little that he was the CEO, and that it would not have mattered to me if he was a government minister. The important fact is I was denied the services I had legitimately paid for. The bus company officials, of course, apologized profusely because they had to choose between an irate customer expressing extreme displeasure at how the situation was handled and a CEO ready to fire them should he not get his desired seat. No matter how much I protested, I lost my seat, and for that matter, missed the important choir meeting I was planning to catch later that evening.

Thankfully enough, the officials at the bus station offered to put me on the same prized seat in a different bus, which, quite surprisingly, filled up in less than ten minutes. As I sat there reminiscing on what ensued, I immediately had the sense that I failed to present a good example as a Christian leader. I started wondering about the possible "what-if's" that might have played themselves out. For example, what if someone attended chapel at the university and heard me speak about showing a good example to all believers and what if that person happened to be at that very bus station, traveling to the same destination, and what if that person actually heard me verbalizing my disgust at how I was treated?

In the midst of all those "what-ifs", a distinct question popped into my mind—a question that was more real than surreal, as follows: "Did you really show a good example in speech? Did you really show a good example in life? Did you really show a good example in love? Did you really show a good example in faith? Did you really show a good example in purity? You have just preached the same sermon in chapel. Did you really live it out in your own personal life" To each one of those questions, of course, I answered in the negative. I knew, at once, that God had put me through the test, and I failed it. I also discovered that even if I had made it to the meeting in time, it was cancelled owing to inclement weather that hindered the smooth flow of traffic in that city. I went through a very short wilderness moment, and failed the test. If I failed the test on such a simple example, would I really be trusted to pass the test when countenancing bigger issues? The test revealed what was in my heart, and I went to the Lord in confession and in prayer.

As noted, however, this test is only a simple one, relatively speaking. God's children face even more severe tests than merely desiring prized-seats in buses. I have already noted, in the introduction, the kinds of tests close friends have lived through. Personally, I have lived through the bitter experience of watching the burial of my brother. I have lived through the bitter experience of burying my father and his two brothers, all of whom died within a span of one year. I will retell this story in greater detail toward the end of this book. At this point, I only note the following: Owing to the closeness with which I spent my life with my own father, his departure and the bitter agony of watching my mother live through the experience will remain forever etched in my memory. The bitterness is accentuated by additional experiences, which I will choose to leave unmentioned in these pages.

What I wish to mention is the nature of the test I encountered as I witnessed their demise. In many ways, the experience made me stronger than I was previously. For some reason, having known that my father's death was only a matter of time, I was unsure of how I would handle the entire scene as it unfolded. I was afflicted with episodes of fear. I wondered if my faith would remain intact in the midst of these. I wondered if my sanity would be sustained. Moreover, since my father, in the spiritual sense, was the glue that cemented our family together, I wondered if, after his death, our family would disintegrate. The fact that our family was scattered all over the country turned out to be a sad reality. Slowly, however, God brought our family together again. Each member of the family experienced his or her own wilderness moment. In a certain sense, God put each one of us through various tests, some of which revealed to us the nature of our hearts, while others brought out an unexplainable sense of resilience.

Of course, as noted, I have omitted some details that would have put this story in a more severe context. Including those details, however, would have taken this work far afield—way beyond my immediate intentions here. My goal in giving this two-fold story, one very recent and the other relatively old, is the fact that I have experienced my share of getting tested in the wilderness moment. This share is perhaps relatively mild, compared to what you, the reader, might have known or what you might be going through currently. What I wish to encourage you, as you read these pages, is the importance of asking yourself the question: Am I going through a wilderness moment? If so, what kind of test am I experiencing, and what goal or purpose is this test trying to fulfill? Sometimes answers are readily available. Sometimes they are not.

Consider, for example, the case presented to a close friend who happened to be giving a talk on this very issue. He had just completed a lecture on the Problem of Evil, namely, on the question of why, if God exists, suffering seems to exist as well. I found my friend's lecture brilliantly presented. After my friend presented his talk, the forum was opened up for a question and answer session. I will never forget the question asked by one attendee at the conference. Her question, if I recall correctly, could be summarized as follows: What possible purposes could God be accomplishing by allowing instances of pointless suffering to afflict his children? Her question narrowed itself down to the question of rape. She wondered what purposes God might try to fulfill by allowing innocent suffering such as rape.

I think my friend tackled the question quite brilliantly, first, by admitting that in some of these instances we may not know the purposes God might be accomplishing, since he has greater knowledge of the overall outworking of the entire universe than we do. What we can believe, however, is the fact that the unfortunate incident of rape did not happen in vain, in the sense that we can trust God to bring some good out of that experience. He admitted, and I commend him for that, that the experience of rape is most certainly a very traumatic thing. However, he noted that the experience of rape did not happen in vain. The other option, of course, is to think that it happened in vain, and this would be a lot more existentially traumatic, for then, we would be assuming the absence of a universal system of justice as well as the absence of an Eternal Judge who would right all wrongs. In the end, no one could be held accountable for the actions in a way that would deter future occurrences.

Could there be a test coming through in such cases? This possibility is logically feasible. The fact that it is a test, however, may not be immediately clear to us. The purpose of the test might be just as inaccessible. What we do know is that the experience, in light of God's overall scheme of things, does not happen in vain, and that God can be trusted to come through even in such instances. Rather than try to speculate about the purposes of these moments, a good beginning would be to go to the Scriptures and see what pointers the Scriptures might give us.

7

THE BIBLICAL TEST

THE BOOK OF Deuteronomy gives us one reason God allowed the Israelites to experience their own version of wilderness moments—to test them. Interestingly, he wanted to test them for a specific purpose, namely to know what was in their hearts. How would this knowledge be acquired? What would be the indicator of the contents of their hearts? According to Deuteronomy 8:2, the indicator was whether or not the Israelites would obey God's commandments.

We are at once faced with a puzzling issue. Is the issue illustrated by the possibility that God did not know whether or not the Israelites would obey his commandments and that, in order for him to acquire this knowledge, he had to take them through the wilderness? Or is the issue illustrated by the possibility that God did, in fact, know what was in their hearts, and that he was, therefore, taking the Israelites through the wilderness in order to expose to the Israelites what was in their hearts?

To answer this question, we will need to borrow from other portions of Scripture that seem to demonstrate that God, in fact, knows the contents of our hearts, not based on some tests he must perform to reveal those contents, but irrespective of whether or not those tests are performed. However, in order to be comprehensive, we might also need to consider those verses in Scripture that seem to indicate that God does not know the contents of our hearts until he puts us through some tests.

Let me begin with the latter view, namely, that God does not know the contents of our hearts until he puts us through certain tests to reveal just those contents. One that comes to mind, immediately, is the story of Abraham and Isaac. Upholders of this view would maintain that God did not know the nature of Abraham's devotion to him prior to putting Abraham to the test. Only after Abraham passed the test of not withholding his son did God know of Abraham's devotion when Abraham expressed a willingness to offer his son as a sacrifice to God. The words of God, immediately after this knowledge was determined, came forth clearly when God said: "Now I know that you fear God, because you have not withheld from me your son, your only son."

I notice that a certain variety of theologians called 'open theists' often refer to this passage as proof of the contention that God does not know the future free acts of his children until they make them. This view seems to place some limits on the doctrine of God's omniscience. I find it incorrect, in light of certain texts such as, for example, the case where Christ knew that Peter would deny him three times before the rooster crowed once. Seemingly, Christ possessed infinite knowledge of Peter's heart, way above what Peter knew. I will return to this passage when presenting the other view alluded to earlier, namely, that God did know the contents of the Israelite's hearts and, therefore, the test was meant for the Israelites, and not meant for God.

How, then should we view the passage referring to God's knowledge of Abraham's devotion? Notice, for example how the utterer is introduced. The speaker of the words in Genesis 22:12 is really introduced as "the angel of the Lord" in Genesis 22:11. This angel, then, seems to be speaking on behalf of God. This lack of knowledge of Abraham's devotion, on the part of the angel of the Lord in Genesis 22:12, can be correctly attributed to angels, who lack omniscience, though, admittedly, remain remarkably more knowledgeable than humans. If this fact gets understood, then the question of the speaker not knowing about Abraham's fear for God becomes less puzzling.

Moreover, as already noted in the case of Peter, the disciple of Jesus, God the Son seems to know the contents of human hearts, and does not need to figure out the nature of those contents by subjecting humans to tests of the sort mentioned in Deuteronomy 8:2. To be sure, this motif is reflected in another passage about Christ's knowledge of the human heart found in the Book of John that says: "He did not need man's testimony about man, for he knew what was in a man."[10] In other words, God the Son already knows the

10 John 2:25

contents of the human heart and does not need to gain additional information about it. Of course, if God the Son knows about the human heart so comprehensively, then, surely, God the Father knows just as much.

This fact, therefore, leaves us to conclude that when God tested the children of Israel in the wilderness, his goal and purpose was to reveal the contents of the human heart to the Israelites. He knew the nature and contents of their hearts already. The test was, therefore, not meant for God the Father. The test was meant for the children of Israel. God wanted them to know the extent of their commitment to obeying the commands of God. If Israel's salvation history is anything to go by (and it is something to go by), the contents of the hearts of the Israelites was forcefully revealed when, for example, they built the Golden Calf when Moses was on Mt. Sinai receiving the ten commandments. Shortly after their salvation from bondage in Egypt, they turned away from the one who delivered them. Moreover, God himself predicted Israel's rebellion as they advanced towards the Promised Land (see Deuteronomy 31:16–18). God could not have predicted this rebellion, which did take place later, if he did not have comprehensive knowledge of the nature of their hearts.

The test God put them under, therefore, was for the purpose of revealing to the Israelites the nature of their hearts. Vowing to follow God was one thing. Actually following God was quite another. The Israelites did vow to follow God. In reality, however, they rebelled against him numerous times. The purpose of the tests they went through in their wilderness moment revealed to the Israelites how vulnerable they were to violating the very vows they made before their God. A similar test was placed before Peter, the disciple of Jesus. He, too, vowed to stay put should Christ's disciples abandon him. For a while he did quite well, until he was challenged to sustain his identity with Christ. At that point, his vows could no longer hold, and he used the same lips to deny his master.

Peter's test, therefore, revealed to Peter the contents of his heart. Without the severity of the test, Peter would not have known the fragility of his devotion to Christ. I suggest that something similar seems to be unfolding in the lives of the Israelites. God put the Israelites to the test in order to reveal to the Israelites the contents of their hearts. In this way, if God were to decide to judge the nation of Israel, he would be justified in his sentence.

8

THE TEST IN JOB'S LIFE

GOLDSMITHS CAN TEACH us a lot about tests. Consider gold smelting—the process by which goldsmiths purify gold. The goldsmiths accomplish this goal by using pressure and heat, and other chemicals as well. Upon the completion of the process, the remaining gold turns out quite pure. According to the goldsmiths, step one of the smelting process involves processing the raw ore wherein the material is pulverized into fine particles, which are then placed into a furnace at temperatures well above the melting point of gold. The goal, at this stage, is to burn off as many impurities in the gold as possible. The next step involves introducing chemicals to facilitate separating the pure gold from other minerals and metals. Upon refining the gold ore and the scrap gold, the gold is returned to the furnace for further smelting. Notice how intense heat seems necessary for the purification of the ore.

When Job was tested, he used this very analogy of gold in his discourse with his friends who tried to console him. Job remarks: "But he knows the way that I take; when he has tested me, I will come forth as gold."[11] Job seemed to draw an analogy between his life and the process of testing and purifying gold. In much the same way gold passes through fire for purification, so did Job feel as if he went through the fiery trials of pain and suffering. He seemed to believe he would come through the trials victoriously and successfully when the trials finally come to an end. Obviously, from this perspective alone, Job took a positive view of his trials. It seemed, to him, a learning process, which we shall revisit in a different section of this work.

From our perspective, however, we have an advantage that Job did not have. We know, for example, of the conversation that ensued in Heaven between God and the enemy. Job, apparently, did not. We know that the enemy came up with the idea of attacking Job in order to get Job to curse God. Again, Job, seemingly, did not know of what was going on in the background. In fact, Job seemed to believe God was the source of his suffering.[12]

This fact seems to point us to an important difference between a test and a temptation. Clearly, the enemy is the source of temptation. God, however, is not the source of temptation. The words of James, the apostle, forcefully underscore this fact that when he says: "When tempted, no one should

---

11 Job 23:10
12 Job 13:15

say 'God is tempting me.' For God cannot be tempted by evil, nor does he tempt anyone."[13]

However, God can be a source of tests, as already noted for the case of Abraham. This fact means the goals of tests introduced into our lives remain quite different from the goals of temptations afflicting us. The tests and trials we face seem aimed at producing greater goods in our lives, goods we would, otherwise, not have. Temptations, on the other hand, seem aimed at enticing us to sin. Logically speaking, then, God would not be the author of temptation, for that would entail getting us to sin against him, the very thing he wishes to expunge from our lives. The enemy, therefore, can be considered the source of temptation. Our own desires, also, can be sources of temptation. James makes this point quite clear as well.[14]

This distinction, however, leaves us wondering whether Job's afflictions were temptations or trials. To the extent that the enemy tried to get Job to curse God, Job's sufferings were temptations. To the extent, however, that Job saw himself as coming forth as gold at the end of his attacks, his sufferings can be considered a test, or a trial. This creates the further observation that some trials really do come as temptations to sin. Job's example is an important case in point.

In what ways, then, would a believer know the difference between the two, and how would a believer make this distinction when either trials or temptations come his or her way?

---

13 James 1:13
14 James 1:14

Perhaps one could get a pointer from Job's life. To the extent the believer finds himself or herself enticed to sin against God in light of the countenanced wilderness moment, he or she might consider the trial a temptation. To the extent that the believer sees, in the wilderness moment, an opportunity for growth and maturity, then the believer might consider the moment a test or a trial.

Admittedly, owing to the intensity or severity of the wilderness moment, the believer may not always be in a position or state of mind to know the difference between the wilderness moment as test and the moment as a temptation. At that time, what the believer wishes to see, or hopes to find, is immediate relief from the pain and suffering. This goal is all that will matter for the believer in such instances. For example, a believer suffering from pain caused by cancer lacks the time to reflect on whether or not the experience comes from the enemy or from God. What the believer wants, at that time, is immediate relief from pain.

Notice that this distinction between trials and temptations meant little to Job throughout his suffering. What Job wanted and what he desired most at that time was something more important, namely, relief from his pain and the assurance of God's presence and control in his life. Job was not interested in philosophical speculations about the nature of his suffering. He wanted immediate relief and God's assuring presence. Still, Job was sure he would be a better person at the end of his trials, suffering, and pain.

The hope that every believer has when living through wilderness moments is this: Every wilderness moment comes to an end. This fact, of course, means that every test also comes to an end. In many cases, it ends in a way that allows the believer to move on with his life, having passed the test with flying colors. In many other cases, the test seems to come to an end in death, allowing the suffering believer to countenance God's face at the end of this world—an experience the apostle Paul calls "better-by-far." The important thing to note, just the same, is that such tests lack an eternal endurance. When tested for a while, we must glory in the fact that the tests will surely come to an end. God is faithful enough to ensure that this end will truly come.

I close this section with a heart-rending story. In one of my preaching engagements in North Carolina, a certain lady walked up to me with a question. She wanted to know how to deal with her brother's sudden tragic death. It mattered little to her that the assurance of Heaven gave the Christian an eternal hope. What she wanted, at that time, was not a major philosophical or theological treatise on how Heaven provided relief from pain, though, of course, I think such truths remain important in our daily lives and discourse. For this reason, she fired one question after another, and I tried my best to answer those questions. What remained unclear to me was whether she needed me to be there for her in a pastoral role, or whether she merely wanted to express her pain and agony over her brother's death. I noticed her tears and anger as she labored through her struggles, and I tried my best to be sensitive to those concerns. Not knowing whether or not I ministered to her, I promised to meet up with her again within the next day of the conference where I was preaching.

Unfortunately, she never showed up, and I ended up not fulfilling the goals I hoped to fulfill as the conference unfolded.

Had I known at that time what I know now, I would have quickly drawn the distinction between giving her a philosophical response and giving her a pastoral response. A believer undergoing the test that a wilderness moment brings needs to be approached pastorally rather than philosophically. The believer needs the assurance of God's presence as he or she walks through the test. At that time, the pastor provides avenues through which God's presence can be countenanced in the inner spirit. Such assurances make it possible for believers to find the test a lot more bearable.

In light of this truth, bear in mind that the children of Israel did not walk through the wilderness on their own. God walked through that experience with them. God walked with them in their struggles, in their trials, as well as in their grumbling. I intend to give this motif a more extended treatment later. For now, I only point out that God never allowed the Israelites to experience their tests all by themselves. God walked with them the entire 40 years. The assurance, here, is that he too, is ready and willing to walk with you through your tests and trials, however long those tests and trials will take. The assurance of God's presence, then, makes the journey through one's wilderness moments, at the very least, bearable, for the simple reason that the believer knows he is not alone in this journey.

PART THREE

THE HUMBLING

9

A LIVING LESSON IN HUMILITY

BESIDES THE TEST motif, a second motif presents itself when one lives through wilderness moments. It is the motif of humility. On two occasions in that passage, Moses points out how God made the Israelites pass through the wilderness for one other purpose. He wanted to humble the Israelites. He wanted the Israelites to know what allowing God to be their provider really means. God tried to accomplish this task among the Israelites in a way that remained totally baffling across the board. In what ways can we say the children of Israel were humbled?

In order to answer this question, let me draw your attention to the importance of humility. Many have noted how humility remains a very rare commodity. The opposite of humility, pride, is found in plenty. Politicians love to be proud. I can speak of pastors, because I am one, and I know how pride continues to bring down ministries and ministers who would, otherwise have been immensely beneficial toward God's kingdom.

As a pastor and, at the same time, a musician, I struggle with this very issue. Whenever I seem to have delivered a sermon I believe was almost a home run, to use baseball language, I end up feeling really good about myself, forgetting, at times, that only God could have made such an experience possible. Whenever I seem to have succeeded in leading a congregation to a heartwarming and toe-tapping plethora of worship, I struggle with the temptation to attribute praise and glory to myself. In all these instances, pride comes to the forefront, taking the position that only God should be taking.

I recall an unfortunate encounter I witnessed concerning pride in my own father's life. He was a well-respected farm manager of a government national farm in Kenya. Relatively speaking, he earned a lot more money than the average Kenyan. He bought himself a huge saloon car, and was a man of many financial means. He lived in a huge home, established himself as a shrewd businessman, and basically made available to us the basic necessities in life. To be sure, in terms of food, clothing and shelter, we seemed to have more than we needed. This achievement made our lives very easy.

Throughout this experience, we had little suspicion that a life of humility, nay, humiliation, was slowly but steadily approaching. A major mistake my father made in his life was his failure to save adequately for his retirement. To be sure, he did save some retirement money. However, upon his retirement, he invested all his money in the motor vehicle transportation business. Unfortunately, and for some completely unexplainable reason, the entire business collapsed right before his very eyes. The motor vehicle he bought had engine failure multiple times, and the business failed to take off as he hoped it would. Trying to put that vehicle on the road was an expensive exercised that used up all of his retirement savings, putting him into additional debt he never anticipated. Getting into debt at his age was one of the most unwise things he did.

He would then find himself settling back in his ancestral home without money, without his business, and only his home to show for what he had built and gathered over those twenty years. Besides this experience, his health failed him. High blood pressure, gouty arthritis and gastro-intestinal ulcers took over his body. He started falling apart right before our very eyes. He settled back in his ancestral home that lacked running water and electricity, the very things he was used to and could not live without while he worked as the manager of the government national farms. We watched him deteriorate physically. He walked with difficulty. Since we had no running water, we had to fetch water from a water-well infested with frogs, mosquito larvae and snakes. The well was anything but hygienic. Instead of using a water system latrine, we settled for an outhouse. Moreover, because my father could not walk whenever his arthritis flared up, we had to give him a ride to the outhouse on a wheelbarrow. Everyday my father was haunted by the height from which he had fallen. He could not believe he had plummeted so drastically. He wondered how he missed the warning signs that pointed to the possibility that he would no longer drive his saloon car, but would watch his own sons wheel him to the outhouse in a wheelbarrow.

Moreover, owing to the fact that he was no longer working, and to the fact that he had used up all his retirement money, he struggled to put bread on the table for us, his children. I remember one evening when he cried like a child upon realizing he could not raise enough money to buy food for our subsistence.

I quickly point out that prior to his fall from grace to grass, my father had little room for God. He knew God existed, and he knew God answered prayers. However, he seemed to have other important issues to attend to. God would only come into the picture when my father felt he needed God. However, as long as he had the financial means, he saw no need for God.

Understandably, then, when my father realized he had fallen flat on his belly financially and that the only place to look was up to Heaven, this fact got his attention. He began to seek God a lot more seriously, quite possibly for the wrong reasons, namely, that God would restore the wealth he had lost. However, he had not made any conscious decision to accept Christ as his Lord and Savior. Seemingly, at one point in his life, he finally surrendered to the Lordship of Christ. The Gospel message finally reached his heart in a way it never did before. At that point he realized Christ was all he needed. Whether he had the wealth or not was no longer his goal in life. His goal in life was to live for Christ. He had to learn to depend on God for just about everything. His life of pride got replaced by a life of humility, a life of discovering that only

God could feed him and provide for him. At a time he could no longer provide for himself, God provided for him. When he could no longer feed himself, God fed him. I wonder if something similar to this lesson might be what the children of Israel had to live through. Let us turn to it.

10

THE BIBLICAL LESSON IN HUMILITY

SEEMINGLY, THE ISRAELITES, too, needed a lesson in humility. They had learned to provide for themselves with their own hands. They knew what it meant to go out in their harsh lives in Egypt and raise their own cattle, grow their own foods and do many activities that would help provide for their daily sustenance. To think that they would have to depend on some other source or power for their sustenance was an exercise beyond this world.

Scripture reminds us that God humbled them in at least two ways. First, he caused them to hunger while they were in the wilderness. Secondly, he fed them with food hitherto unknown to either them or their fathers. God put them in a situation where they had to come to terms with their hunger. Since they were in the desert they lacked the resources to provide for themselves. They could not find any water there. They were unable to locate any zones that had any crops or additional foods.

While they wondered where they could find the relevant supplies for their foods, and after they had grumbled to Moses about the lack of foods they experienced at that time, God decided to surprise them. From the sky he provided them with manna. Neither the Israelites nor their fathers possessed prior knowledge of the kind of food they were picking up daily for their sustenance. Where they could not provide for themselves, God stepped in and provided for them in a very miraculous way.

This experience forced them to know that their provider was God. Only God could truly provide for their physical and spiritual needs. In and of themselves, they seemed completely and totally incapable to make those very provisions. The fact that they were in the desert made the situation worse. For this reason, their incapability was accentuated in a way unknown to them. The situation was made worse by the fact that they were in a desert. However, they learned an important lesson here. Even when they were in a place as dry as a desert, God still provided for them in meaningful and powerful ways.

This lesson was not limited to the Israelites alone. The case of Prophet Elijah and the widow of Zarephath is one that provides an excellent example. When all the food seemed to have run out in Israel from a drought that, apparently, had been caused by God, God was still able to provide for Elijah, and for the widow of Zarephath.[15] It was a lesson the widow had to learn.

Providing for oneself when resources seem plenty is one thing. However, providing for oneself amidst scarcity

---

15 1 Kings 17:1

is staggering. Even more staggering—though in a positive way—is the fact that God can provide for his children even when his children seem completely unable to provide for themselves. Until his children reach the point of knowing this, they will always hesitate to allow God to provide for them, and they will try to supply their own needs by their on hands.

God, however, wants us to express absolute trust and dependence on him to provide for us, whether we live in plenty or live in scarcity. The question, then, is not whether we can trust God to provide for us in the midst of plenty alone; rather, it is whether we can trust him to provide for us whether we live in plenty or live in scarcity. This seems to be the heart of the matter when taking our lesson in humility—absolute dependence on God whether in plenty or scarcity.

This fact seems significant for current trends in the Western world. The very fact that the West remains persistently and consistently in the midst of plenty gives a majority of them the tendency to believe that they alone, and no one else, made it possible for them to reach that level of self-sufficiency. A lot of their achievements get attributed to their ability to invent superior products and gadgets in their technological disciplines. God's role in bringing the West to this point of plenty in their lives continues to get ignored, and sometimes, trashed. God is no longer seen to play the role in the lives of individuals in the previous past. To be sure, God, the Bible, and Christianity continue to be viewed as stumbling blocks to further scientific inquiry and should, therefore, be expressed only in one's private life.

However, when one crosses the ocean from the Western world into the Global South, and especially into the African continent, one finds a different scenario. The situation in certain places in Africa continues to depict a willingness, on the part of the contemporary African, to pledge allegiance to God on a regular basis. In the midst of scarcity, many African Christians find themselves ready and willing to acknowledge a higher power, namely, God, as the one responsible for their daily living and sustenance. They remain keenly aware of their utter helplessness in the absence of God and of their complete dependence on God in their daily lives. This awareness creates, for the African, the sense of humility quite absent in many arenas in the Western world.

The financial recession of recent years in the United States of America, however, seemed to bring many to the realization that they really do not hold much stake in their financial future. They discovered how their entire lifetime of savings can be wiped out in very real ways—ways neither they nor the authorities in government could control. As already noted, this fact played itself out so fiercely, leading some individuals to commit suicide upon seeing almost all their savings go down the drain in the volatile financial market.

The state of affairs was a moment of humility for many. Some previously well-to-do individuals found themselves lining up for food stamps. The individuals lived affluent lives. Finding themselves lining up for food stamps seemed an affront on their ego. They struggled through this realization, and expressed their complete distrust of the Washington politicians. In short, they lived through a moment of humility. Of course this reality was and still is rather troubling.

The children of Israel lived through a similar experience. One will recall their complaint about having no food in the wilderness. Very quickly, they forgot their misery in Egypt, longing for the varieties of foods they once ate even while in bondage. They remembered how they were still able to feed themselves in spite of the harsh conditions of slavery. Suddenly, in the wilderness, they countenanced a condition they thought was worse than slavery—hunger and thirst. It seemed a humiliating experience for them.

God, in his gracious mercy provided food for them where it seemed no longer available. He gave them water where they seemed unable to find some. According to the text in question, God brought them into this very situation to remind them, quite importantly, that irrespective of how severe the situation seemed, he could still provide for them in remarkable ways. This fact was, so to speak, a lesson worth learning for all of them. The lesson itself seemed focused on an important motif, namely: Humility is a state in which you come to the realization that your gifts, abilities and talents can only go so far in sustaining you, and that God, the facilitator of these gifts, abilities and talents, is the only one capable of taking you where your own self cannot. Coming to terms with this reality remains at the heart of the virtue of humility—a discovery each one of us will have to countenance at some point in our lives.

This enunciates the reason a close friend of mine always rebuked me when he sensed instances of pride in my heart.

He regularly reminded me of how important it was for me to remain down on my knees in humility if I ever wished to see God lifting me up in his own time. He reminded me that the only way to remain constantly lifted up by God is to remain down on my knees. The lesson stuck with me for a long time. Whether or not I have consistently applied it in my life, of course, is another story altogether!

11

THE HUMBLING EXPERIENCE OF JOB

INTERESTINGLY, THIS NOTION of humility featured quite unmistakably in Job's life. One must bear in mind that, prior to his sufferings, Job was an extremely wealthy man, in possessions of thousands of heads of livestock. Seemingly, he employed numerous servants who helped him manage his wealth. He also was a very respectable family man and very devout, earning the praise of God. The sufferings he endured brought him into a low position, one he did not anticipate, but accepted when he realized he came into this world without anything, and would get out of this world, equally, without anything.[16]

In what ways, then, do we see evidence of humility in Job's life? We can decipher this fact from numerous passages in the Book of Job. The first of these finds important

---

16 Job 1:20–22

mention in the very words already alluded to above. Having enough insight to note that he came into this world without anything and that he would leave this world without anything, Job's alternative was to offer praise to God. He seemed to think, quite rightly, that only God can be exalted under such circumstances, recognizing that God is the provider as well as the one who allows our resources to run out. This, in itself, seems to be a lesson in humility. The lesson in humility does not stop here. Additional passages in the book expose us to the severity of the humility that came about in Job's life.

Consider, for example, Job's short description of his ill-health when he says: "My body is clothed with worms and scabs, my skin is broken and festering."[17] In other words, he who happened to be of perfect health, and wore fine clothing, could only look at the boils, and worms, and broken skin, and festering skin, all of which replaced his clothes. In other words, his humble state was underscored by the fact that a skin disease replaced his elegant clothing. Much later in that chapter, Job would speak of the only comfort he hoped to get from his suffering. However, even here, he was afflicted by anguish in his spirit and terrifying nightmares. The severity of his physical affliction led him to prefer death to enjoying his physical bodily life.

The third aspect of humility experienced by Job is the very idea of his reputation. His own words attest to this fact as follows: "I have become a laughing stock to my friends, though I called upon God and he answered—a mere laughing stock,

---

17 Job 7:5

though righteous and blameless"[18] Later, echoing a similar theme, Job re-states it even more forcefully as follows: "God has made me a byword to everyone, a man in whose face people spit.[19] Still, the following words depict an even more graphic form of humility:

> "He has alienated my brothers from me; my acquaintances are completely estranged from me. My kinsmen have gone away; my friends have forgotten me. My guests and my maidservants count me a stranger; they look upon me as an alien. I summon my servant but he does not answer, though I beg him with my own mouth. Even the little boys scorn me; when I appear they ridicule me. All my intimate friends detest me; those I love have turned against me. I am nothing but skin and bones; I have escaped with only the skin of my teeth.[20]

In these words Job captures the humbling experience of having his reputation ruined.

Of course more examples can be found in the book of Job than these three. However, I draw attention to these three as a way of illustrating how Job lived through the important lesson of humility. He recognizes his inability to do anything

---

18 Job 12:14
19 Job 17:6
20 Job 19:13–20

for himself. Shortly after receiving the news about the death of his children and the loss of his wealth, he acknowledged the fact that he lacked the power to bring any possessions into this world. Moreover, he lacked the power to take any possessions out of this world.

I find this acknowledgement a brutal reminder of the realities we face in life. For some reason, we find ourselves buying into the notion of taking our possessions with us beyond the grave. As Job has reminded us, no wealth amassed this side of Heaven will follow us into our next life. We leave all our possessions behind, including our homes, only to be lowered six feet under the ground, no longer capable of laying hold of anything we owned while still alive. As I will show in chapter twelve, once we face this state of affairs along with its implications, we confront a staggering reality.

I also noted earlier in this section how Job's failing health presented itself as an opportunity for humility for Job. Seemingly, he was afflicted with an extremely severe and ugly skin disease, enough to make anyone turn his or her face away from Job. The disease, and the effects of its attack on Job, was revolting, both to the victim and the beholder. No one could stand the sight presenting itself in the person of Job. The experience was hellish in every way.

This story reminds me of an experience in my teenage years that will remain forever etched in my memory. Though significantly less severe than Job's experience, I find it illustrative of the reaction from Job's friends. The experience started quite innocuously. My mother was entertaining a guest, and my brother and I were seated in the living room of the house, basically doing nothing, except for the intermittent moments of reading a book here, and a newspaper there while listening to the music over the radio. I decided to sit outside at the verandah of the house, playing my father's old guitar. My two sisters, out of sheer desire to do something worthwhile, decided to fetch firewood for the fireplace that evening. As I sang through that morning, suddenly both sisters starting screaming and yelling at the top of their voices. Obviously, something was wrong. I put my guitar aside, or more accurately, threw it aside and started running in their direction. Phyllis, my elder sister was running in the direction of the house, still yelling at the top of her lungs. I asked her what the problem was, and she mumbled something about my other sister, Lillian, who could not run because the axe injured her toe. Immediately after seeing the gory sight, I turned my face away from it so violently I almost hurt my neck. What I saw was revolting. We knew it was only a matter of time before my sister would lose her toe. In no time, we were able to rush my sister to hospital. The doctors could not save her toe. After a long, meticulous surgery, the doctors grafted her foot skin over the wound.

Knowing that my sister would live the rest of her life without her toe troubled me deeply. Of course, the experience was a brutal reminder of how vulnerable we remain to injuries from the world around us. It was a reminder to us of our frailties and our weaknesses. In short, it put us in our place with decisive firmness. It was a humbling experience.

In a certain sense, the enemy was trying to put Job in his place. He was trying to show Job that God was not the kind of caring person Job took him to be. Moreover, the enemy wanted Job to look as revolting as possible in the eyes of the world. A person who falls this low from a state of pristine health would no longer hold the highly regarded position of *counselor* among his fellow citizens, which he was. Not only was the experience humiliating for Job, it was humbling. His pride, as the custodian of wisdom among his peers, was wounded.

The pride I refer to here, is not the sinful pride of trying to elevate oneself above everyone. Rather, it is the reasonable pride of expressing pleasure over one's achicvcmcnts, such as the kind of pride parents would have over their child for excelling in school. Job's friends seemed to have been proud of Job's achievement.[21] However, upon seeing Job's ill health, that kind of pride eroded, and it led them to assume Job must have sinned against God. Job's reputation, as already noted, also suffered a setback. Sin, for Job's friends, was the only explanation for Job's suffering. At any rate, Job found himself on the defensive, pleading with God to show up and vindicate him in the end.

In short, it was a humiliating experience for Job. One might ask: How, then, would Job benefit from this humbling experience? To answer this question, one need not look further than the *actual* fact that Job was humbled. Humility is, on the whole, better than pride. Humility is the passage toward elevation by God. We get this fact from Scripture that

---

21 See, for example, Job 4:3,4

God will lift the one who remains humble.[22] One will notice that through this very path of humility, though extremely harsh and undesirable, God lifted Job in the end. God blessed Job with better health, better wealth, and more children fairer than previous ones. This experience, we are reminded, consoled Job. It was an experience worth living through, even though humility was really not the reason Job suffered; rather, it seemed to be a by-product of his suffering. I now turn to the next aspect.

---

22 See 1 Peter 5:7

12

THE GREAT HUMBLER

I STATED, IN AN earlier section, how humility entails, in a fundamental way, coming to the realization that our personal gifts, abilities and talents can only take us so far, and that only God, the facilitator of those gifts and talents, remains the only person capable of taking us beyond the abilities of those gifts and talents. I wish to pursue this notion further, in light of the many deceptions we live with in our daily lives.

Without question, we have abilities to accomplish different tasks and objectives in our lives, from the very simple task of waking up in the morning, to the more difficult task of producing some of the most sophisticated technologies previously unknown to us. This ability to do things autonomously gives us a false sense of invincibility. Most of us wake up every morning taking quite for granted our ability to move our bodies at will. We assume that possessing such an ability is, indeed, a given.

We forget that powerful reminder from the apostle Paul that only in God do we live and move and have our being.[23] Paul reminds us, here, that our very ability to do *anything* is, itself, powered by God. All he needs to do is to withdraw that ability to move in us, in order for us to realize how vulnerable we remain to states of helplessness. That fact, almost always, needs to be underscored in our lives. Unfortunately, we forget how vulnerable we are to such situations. We forget, for example, the importance of thanking God on a daily basis for sustaining our lives each day, each night, each morning and each evening. Only when accosted by potentially life-threatening illnesses do we realize how vulnerable we are to such weaknesses.

However, even when we fall sick in such situations, we still remain indifferent to the fact that our very being depends, quite fundamentally, on God's power. Instead of turning to God first to lift us up from our weaknesses, we immediately run to the medicine cabinet, or to the doctor, to see if he or she can restore our health back to us. Unfortunately, doctors, as good as they are (and I remain thankful for their availability), can go only so far in helping to restore our health in many instances. They, too, reach a point where they throw in the towel in resignation, telling us of how difficult it would be to have them find a cure for the diseases afflicting us.

The more we depend on our abilities to sustain ourselves without acknowledging God's power behind those abilities, the prouder we become and the less we feel our need for God.

---

23 See Acts 17:28

The more we acknowledge God's power behind our abilities to do what we would, ordinarily, not do, the humbler we become and the more we will feel our need for God.

A person immobilized completely by a specific illness knows this truth very well. When my family relocated to Orlando, Florida, from Wilmore, Kentucky, we felt as if we were beginning our lives afresh. One of the things this move involved was the challenging exercise of finding new friends. We did not know how this would play itself out. At any rate, rather than being intentional at looking for friends, I chose to let the 'waters of friendship find their own level.'

One afternoon, while preparing to provide the music for a conference held at my workplace, a group of men stood outside the front desk by our office. Upon introducing myself to them, they asked me what my area of specialization was. Upon discovering how I work in the area of philosophy, one of the guests took special interest in me. He seemed hungry for stuff like that. He told me of his teaching experience in Sunday School, and how he incorporates the thinking of important Christian philosophers and theologians from Augustine to current philosophers. The exchange started a friendship that has lasted to this day. However, from the very day we first introduced ourselves to each other, we began to meet regularly over lunch to discuss the thinking of these philosophers, and how their thought patterns continue to influence theological thinking. My friend's desire for knowledge remains insatiable. His hunger for information in theology would put many students of theology to shame.

At one point my friend stopped communicating. For some reason, the fact that he had stopped communicating had not impressed itself on me until I happened to see a text he sent me weeks before. At that point I felt I needed to call him to find out what he had been up to for the past couple of weeks. What he shared on the other end of the line shocked me. He had just suffered a stroke, not long after burying his brother. What surprised me is the fact that this friend had no signs of potentially suffering a stroke. He had been, relatively speaking, in very good health. He exercised regularly. He watched what he ate. Thus, hearing about his stroke shocked me to the core. Thankfully, however, the episode was a mild one. I quickly stopped by his house just to pray with him. As we were talking before praying, he asked me a question whose answer I could not provide immediately because I did not know the answer. He asked: "How much control do we have over our bodies?"

I wondered why he asked me this question. If we have no control of the aging process, or the kinds of sicknesses that afflict us, or even when we come into this world, and yet we know that what we eat affects how we age, and how we take care of our bodies affects the kind of health we will eventually have, where does our control begin and end, and where does nature take over? That question turned out quite humbling for me, owing to the fact that I really could not think of a good answer.

I bring this story to your attention to underscore an important fact: Besides the humility that comes from knowing how little control we have over our bodies, even more humbling is the onset of what each one of us must eventually face—death. I call it the great humbler. It is the only fact antithetical to human survival. From the moment we enter this world, to the point at which we bid it farewell, the fight for our survival begins. Ultimately, it is the fight against dying. We do our best to avoid it. We muster all efforts to keep it at bay. The more we seem to succeed, the prouder we get. Eventually, it begins to catch up with us, whether through aging, through sickness, or through some unanticipated tragic or catastrophic event. It gets the better of us, leading us to a point of complete surrender. In other words, it brings us down to our knees in humility, at the full realization that we remain eternally helpless before it, and completely at its mercy. It is the great humbler because it conquers the rich and the poor, the mighty and the weak, the famous and the infamous. All must contend with what a famous author called "the great equalizer."

In what other ways would death, the great equalizer, also be the great humbler? Death is the great humbler because it destroys every ingredient that feeds and fuels our pride. At death, our abilities dissipate, our credentials become irrelevant, and we evacuate the world we know and become ushered into the world of memories—only memories, into the hearts of people. We remain completely immobile, and rather than walk on the surface of the earth, we must now be located several feet below the surface of the soil. To fall onto the ground is quite humbling. But to be positioned several feet underground in burial, never again to be seen as before, seems worse than "quite humbling." It seems "truly humbling." If this way is how we end up, then it continues to underscore the humbling and humiliating nature of death.

The good news for the believer, however, is that things need not be seen in this way. The believer can admit that death is a truly humbling experience, but the believer need not stop here for at least one reason—the believer rests his or her faith on someone who conquered the grave. He knows that when he dies, he does not leave the land of the living to go to the land of the dying. Rather, he leaves the land of the dying to go to the land of the living, and this is made possible by Christ's resurrection. His resurrection brings hope to a person who truly comes to terms with the humiliating nature of death, and places his hope on the one who conquered the grave. Perhaps, the fact is when living through wilderness moments, the sufferer can hope for redemption by Christ even in the midst of the humbling experience. These moments, though humbling, do not overcome the reality of Christ's victory.

Where does this state of affairs leave us? Consider, first, how humbling wilderness moments have been to you. Think of how, in such instances, you begin recalling your former abilities—how you used to walk with swiftness and run like a gazelle and climb stairways without grabbing your chest in exhaustion. Think of how the formerly good things you experienced in the past continue to elude you in the present. Think of how former relationships no longer exist in your life. You then begin comparing those moments of great agility, great relationships and good graces, with your current state of relative powerlessness, impotence, emptiness and perhaps, grief. The wonderful news about these realities seems to be that they will not haunt you forever. You always have the hope of being released from your inabilities at some point in future, even if the great humbler finally stands at the doorstep of your life and knocks on it.

Whereas you will do well to acknowledge your state of humility, recognizing that you can do nothing by yourself and that you can do all things only through Christ who gives you the strength,[24] you will do even better to acknowledge that God will strengthen you through your weaknesses. He will, in some way, redeem what seems irredeemable in your life, and restore what seems beyond repair. Even more importantly, is the truth that, someday, God will raise our lowly bodies in his Son, Christ Jesus, when death finally gets conquered. My next line will sound paradoxical, but for the Christian, it remains eternally true, that some day, in the not too distant future, even death will die. Revelation 21:4 gives us this assurance. In that sense, God in Christ, conquered the grave for us. The great humbler will, on that day, be truly humbled through obliteration by God's power. This fact is a hope no other system of belief can offer with such boldness. It is a hope you and I should consider a foundation for eternal joy.

---

24 Philippians 4:13

PART FOUR

THE LESSON

13

MY DEPENDENCE ON GOD

WHEN MY FAMILY relocated to Orlando, Florida, from Wilmore, Kentucky, God seemed to have some specific lessons for me. My life has evolved over the years, from the time I watched over my father's cattle and sheep in rural Kisumu, through the time I enrolled as a student of theology at what, at that time, was called Scott Theological College. Having retired from work, and lost all his savings, my father could no longer provide for us, his family, as effectively as he did before. I remember the days and nights we would spend without food, without kerosene to light up the lamps at night, and without enough funds to buy cleaning materials.

This fact may sound unthinkable to individuals living in a culture such as the one we find in the United States, specifically because electric power seems a basic necessity anyone should have. However, having no kerosene to light up the room on any evening, leave alone having a power blackout caused by some storm passing by, remains unfathomable. This reality, plays itself out in the lives of a considerable majority in the Global South, of which I consider myself a progeny. At any rate, living from one day to another was, and continues to be, for some of my family members, an experience of living from hand to mouth, so to speak.

At that time, we would spend more than one hour every day having our family devotions. The devotions began with prayer, followed by singing at least four hymns from a Swahili hymnal, a brief exposition of Scripture, a reciting of *The Lord's Prayer*, and a final prayer, often pleading with God to give us daily our daily bread. The daily experience at home brought our family together in remarkable ways, in spite of finding ourselves smack in the middle of scarcity. At least we had one another.

In a very real sense, we lived through the wilderness, and those wilderness moments brought us on our knees in surrender to God and in total dependence on God. We knew how lost we would be if we were not on God's side. What made our wilderness experience worse was the fact that we lived in the midst of adversity. However, for the sake of protecting those involved in those adversarial goals against our family, I will leave that fact unexplained. Still, knowing how unfavorable our financial situation was, and how hostile to our well-being our immediate environment was, we turned to God, quite unreservedly, for help.

That lesson on dependence on God followed me through college. After gaining acceptance at Scott Theological College as a student, I knew I was incapable of raising the funds to put me through my theological training. It turned out to be a faith venture. On the first day of my arrival at the school, the authorities sent me home for lack of fees. The days that followed my stay at home from school were punctuated with intense prayer and fasting, including setting out the fleece, after the pattern of Gideon in the book of judges. Finally, in answer to my prayers, God came through miraculously, and raised every single cent I needed for my studies at Scott.

Upon completing my studies at Scott College, I interviewed for a youth pastor position at Africa Inland Church (AIC) Jericho in Nairobi. Even when I ministered at AIC Jericho, God continued to provide for me. He used AIC Jericho to raise a good chunk of the funds I needed for further studies in the United States, and provided for my education every step of the way, including using Jimtown United Methodist Church in Lexington, Kentucky, which I previously did not know about, to raise funds for my daily living. They asked me to be their pastor, and supplied my financial needs for seminary. I returned to Kenya for a pastoral ministry at AIC Jericho in Nairobi for one year. While at AIC Jericho, I was accepted at the University of Kentucky's doctoral program to major in philosophy on a full scholarship. In retrospect, I only can say my studies at the University of Kentucky were all funded by God's personal provision. Every step of the way, I learned the importance of depending on God.

While continuing with my post-graduate education at the University of Kentucky, God kept teaching me this lesson. On one occasion, which I have written about in a different book, I sat in class, pondering the aftermath of the collapse of the Twin Towers in New York shortly after two planes flew into those buildings. All students, including me, remained seated, petrified over the television footage of the event as it unfolded. What amazed me was the reaction from my philosophy teacher. He was a self-proclaimed atheist. This fact made his response to the event extremely interesting. He sat there calling on the name of Jesus several times after long pauses of helplessness. Strangely, he faulted all individuals who seemed to subscribe to some form of belief in a Supreme Being. Under the same breath he called out on the name of Christ as a way of expressing his dismay of what kept unfolding through the television screens. I wondered why this professor found it necessary to call on Jesus while rejecting everything represented by that name. Clearly, that gesture seemed to entail a contradiction.

Much later, while still trying to complete my studies at the University of Kentucky, a friend of mine invited me to speak at a conference in Maryland. On our way back from the speaking engagement, we had a connecting flight through Detroit, Michigan. The flight was delayed due to inclement weather. A storm was passing through, and for the sake of safety, the authorities concerned decided to delay all outgoing flights. I imagined they would, also, suspend, for a little while, all incoming flights.

After about ten minutes of waiting for the storm to pass through, our flight was cleared for takeoff. It was a small plane of about fifty passengers. Immediately after takeoff, the clouds around us looked gray and ugly. Suddenly, without warning, the plane flew into dangerously rough air. The storm tossed the plane violently from one side to the other. It was the most turbulent ride my wife and I ever encountered on any single flight. We did not think we would walk out of that plane alive. What amazed me, though, was the fact that almost every passenger in that plane called on the name of Jesus. Everyone was praying for safety. They knew they had to call on the one who could calm the storm. Meanwhile, we had this morbid fear that, perhaps, the plane would break apart. It did not. When we finally landed in Lexington Kentucky, a sigh of great relief and thankfulness filled the air. We were happy to step on solid ground once again.

I draw attention to these two stories to underscore the fact that deep down within each person, we remain aware of our helplessness without God, and our need for him. We remain aware of our complete and total dependence on God. Sometimes we forget this truth. However, every once in a while, God puts us or allows us to countenance situations where this truth finds expression. My life at Asbury Theological Seminary and at the University of Kentucky was punctuated with these lessons.

When I was finally interviewed to teach at Asbury Theological Seminary on a full-time basis, the importance of that lesson began to take a backseat. Rather than continuing with this wonderful virtue of depending on God, I began to lose the importance of asking God to give me, each day, my daily bread. After all, now that I was fully employed, I knew that my daily bread was guaranteed. Since I know I had something to look forward to at the end of every month, I did not have to plead with God to supply my needs anymore. I fully believe God created the opportunity for me to work at Asbury. In that sense, he was already providing for my family and me. However, complacency can soon arise from this kind of set up, where a paycheck seems guaranteed every month, and it might result in not seeing the fact that God is really behind those provisions. When this myopia happens, one remains at risk of forgetting how one should fully depend on God. One then begins to depend on the employee, rather than on God, for one's provisions.

This lesson came forcefully on me as we relocated campuses, from Asbury Seminary's Wilmore Campus in Kentucky, to their campus in Orlando, Florida. Nothing had changed in terms of the paycheck. The school played its part in ensuring our smooth transition to Florida. They funded the move. They helped us re-settle in Florida. However, what we remained unprepared for was the high cost of living the state of Florida demands on its residents compared to the relatively mild cost of living in Kentucky. Moreover, my son and I experienced some unprecedented health issues that wiped out our entire insurance and subsequent savings.

In short, I found myself running to God for help. I could not run to the school for help anymore. The school had played its full part. In running to God for help, it dawned on me how long I had taken before asking God to supply my needs. As if God was walking me through the process, I discovered how I had not prayed that specific prayer from the time I got employed by Asbury until the time I was on my knees asking for God's help. I had depended on the school to provide for me, and had not seen the need to pray for God's provisions. In a gentle but firm and painful rebuke, God reminded me never, ever, to forget where I came from, and always to remember that I depended on him in everything, including the area of seeking him to give me, each day, my daily bread. More than anything, the harshness with which my health temporarily deteriorated jolted me back to my senses. I was no longer the invincible individual I had deluded myself into believing. I continue to learn this lesson, daily, often being reminded how my life remains dependent on God.

That fact is a lesson the children of Israel had to learn. God gives us a snapshot of how he wanted them to learn the importance of depending on God. The full story, of course, is accessible in the book of Exodus. Its summary finds expression in the very text under consideration in this book, to which I now turn.

14

THE ISRAELITE LESSON ON DEPENDENCE

THE BOOK OF Deuteronomy 8:3 comes with an idea worth bearing in mind, namely, the idea of dependence on God. According to Moses, God allowed the children of Israel to go to the land of Canaan via the desert in order for them to learn an important lesson. He wanted them to learn how humans ought not to live on bread alone, but on every word that proceeded from the mouth of God. That lesson, for the entire Israelite community, could only be learned in the Wilderness. Consider his words: "He humbled you, causing you to hunger, and then feeding you with manna, which neither you nor your forefathers had known, to teach you that man does not live on bread alone, but on every word that proceeds from the mouth of God."[25]

All their lives, the Israelites had learned to provide for their own needs with their own hands in the midst of

---

25 Deuteronomy 8:3

extremely harsh conditions of slavery. They provided for their own needs through torture, through the demands of their task-masters, through lack of comfort, and through almost every difficulty a life of slavery could present to them

Just the same, the situation in the desert, though of a much freer quality, seemed tougher than what they experienced in Egypt in the sense that food remained continually unavailable there. They could not provide for themselves even if they wanted to do so. As I have already noted, one will recall how they complained about not having any food for themselves, and how they longed for the meat they ate in Egypt. That longing for the food they had during slavery seemed enough to put them on some kind of a collision course with God, especially the complaint they brought against Moses.

God was up to something. He was preparing them for a very important lesson. He wanted them to know how, in the midst of scarcity, God could give them plenty, in the midst of drought, God could quench their thirst, and in the midst of hunger, God could fill their stomachs. All in all, they learned the importance of relying and depending on God for their daily provisions. The lesson was a difficult one to learn because they learned it in the harsh conditions of the desert. Still, they did learn the lesson. They knew God was their provider.

One of the key lessons found in the midst of wilderness moments is that of dependence on God. Not only does the lesson expose us to the other side of humility, it exposes us to avenues of faith never before anticipated. For example, believing that God often meets our needs is one thing. Actually taking the step to apply this belief in our lives continues to be challenging. Believing, in theory, that God would take care of my wife as she battles the all-dreaded disease known as cancer has, hitherto, been one thing. However, actually taking a step of faith and applying that belief in my wife's current situation was an extremely difficult move on my part. I have come to appreciate the difficulty involved in taking a step of faith. Taking the step of faith often feels, to the skeptic, an easy way out for those unwilling to live through the rigors of reason. I am discovering more and more that such a view of faith seems erroneous. Taking a step of faith toward God with respect to matters as weighty as cancer has been an extremely difficult thing to do—one that takes a lot of courage on the part of the believer. As a philosopher, I can now say with certainty that believing something based on reason seems a lot easier than believing that thing based on faith. I continue to "catch myself" levitating toward the easy activity of trying to reason through my wife's situation in an attempt to figure out what the most rational course of action might be. Ever so often an inner voice reminds me to remain constantly in prayer. I have done so—sometimes eagerly, but at other times without as much eagerness. Still, I continue to pray. I continue to rely on God, trusting him to carry my family through this difficult journey.

One will recall how God demanded total devotion from the Israelites. Having saved them from bondage in Egypt, God was blunt enough to remind the Israelites to depend fully on him rather than on false gods. It happened to be the very first commandment he passed on to them through

Moses. Moreover, in order to ensure continuous devotion to him as their provider, God literally showered food from Heaven, which they ate and were satisfied. Still, we also know how we can lose the significance of such miraculous events.

Consider, for example, how the Israelites longed for a different kind of food than what they knew as manna, and began to crave the meat they left behind, much to God's anger.[26] Not only were they rejecting what God had to offer; they were trying to replace it with an alternative they encountered while in bondage in Egypt. However, throughout their walk, God never relented from underscoring the importance of all his people expressing, in word and deed, their full and total dependence on him. You and I ought to take this lesson seriously, as I will demonstrate in the next section.

---

26 Numbers 11:1–10

15

THE NEED FOR DEPENDENCE

SHORTLY BEFORE DEFENDING my dissertation at the University of Kentucky, I had a discussion with one of my dissertation examiners. He was, and still is, an agnostic. An agnostic, according to how this examiner defines it, is the view that one cannot tell whether or not God exists. That view surprised me, but I was always curious to know how this friend would defend his agnosticism. He never quite gave me an argument in defense of his view, but he did make his position well known to me and to my fellow classmates.

On one occasion, while sitting out for lunch with him, this friend made a startling comment. While insisting on what he considered credible reasons for his agnosticism, he explained how humans seem to be under the jurisdiction of powers beyond their control, and they seemed powerless to escape this fact. Whether or not such powers of nature encapsulated the idea of God, he argued, no one could really tell.

His admission that humans seem to be under the power of forces beyond their control, seemed startling. He seemed to admit how, fundamentally speaking, humans remain helpless without being dependent on some higher power. They remain, indeed, more helpless than one would want us to think.

This fact finds an important illustration whenever we consider how the need for a savior comes sharply into focus as we find ourselves in the middle of crises. The temptation to rush to the scene in order to rescue our fellow human victims drives us to extreme levels. Take the case of Hurricane Katrina in New Orleans, or the tsunami in Japan and Indonesia. Humanitarianism took over, and nations began to send in aid to help the victims.

Consider, also, the crisis in Rwanda. It provoked international outrage, leaving those with a sense of benevolence wondering how the crisis could be solved, and who could step in to help solve the crisis. The international world turned to the then United Nations secretary general for suggestions on how to solve the crisis. Bear in mind how, over the years, the United Nations Organization has been the preferred option for providing solutions to such situations. Unfortunately, as soon as the United Nations secretary general countenanced the crisis, he found himself at a loss for words, and for all practical purposes, at a loss for possible solutions. This failure on the part of the United Nations Organization turned out quite tragic, for it opened the door for blood to get spilled without restraint. Throughout the crises, the international community desperately searched for a solution—a savior to rescue the victims from nationwide slaughter. No savior could be found, and hundreds of thousands of souls died in that tragic civil war.

Therefore, perhaps we should ask: What happens in instances where no matter how much we try to help, nothing can really be done to avert the crisis? At the time of writing this book, a Malaysian Airline Jet has been missing for over two years, probably lost somewhere in the Indian Ocean. Only recently did pieces of evidence in the form of ocean debris begin to emerge, raising hopes that the wreckage of this plane would eventually be found. Relentless searching continues to yield little results, though we cannot rule out the possibility that someday the search teams will locate the jet. Of course, victims and families of these victims continue to express the hope of finding their loved ones. I assume this hope finds expression from the rest of the world through prayers for the location of the plane and the victims.

Notice how such expressions, namely, the exercise of prayer, underscore our need for dependence on something higher than ourselves—something similar, and I dare say, identical, to the Judeo-Christian God. Prayer is always an admission on our part of how our personal efforts can only go so far, and how we need something more powerful than ourselves to take the lead in lifting us up from our crises. The request placed before the United Nations secretary general to step in and arrest the Rwandan crisis was some form of prayer. However, it was addressed to a human being, or to a body that found itself woefully incapable of dealing with the situation. This incapacity brings about a state of helplessness on our part; it brings about our realization that we need this power beyond us to restore the brokenness accosting us.

In such instances we remain keenly aware of our vulnerabilities as humans. We begin to realize how reliant we are on powers above us, and we desperately hope such powers remain cognizant of our condition, our nature as sentient beings. We feel they should come to us as personal rather than impersonal forces, for we know how impersonal forces remain pitifully incapable of understanding the human condition. In addition, we feel as if they should demonstrate some form of benevolence, wherein they come to us with dispositions sympathetic to the concerns of the human heart. What reasons, therefore, do we have, to believe that the higher power might, in a very literal sense, possess some of the positive qualities we have as humans? By positive qualities I refer to the sort of attributes and characteristics that advance our well-being, making us more akin to how we were designed as humans.

In order to answer this question, consider, for example, philosopher Jerry Walls' correct observation that God would not create us with the sort of personhood we possess as humans if God himself were not personal.[27] In the book of Psalms, God brings this very issue to our attention when he asks the following rhetorical questions in Psalm 94:9: "Does he who implanted the ear not hear? Does he who formed the eye not see?" With these questions God reminds us of the fact that the positive qualities we have in our human nature can also be found in God in a very real way. In other words, God, for example, would not bestow upon us the sort of

---

27 Walls, Jerry. *Heaven: The Logic Of Eternal Joy* (New York: Oxford University Press, 2002), 23.

benevolent qualities we possess if he himself were not benevolent. Analogous remarks can be made about his moral qualities, as well as his quality as a personal God.

Let me, then, reconsider the notion of benevolence, that is, the desire to act kindly and in a loving way both to those we cherish and treasure as well as to those with whom we lack relatively close ties. The very existence of this desire, I would suggest, points us to the very issue of our dependence on one another. If we did not need each other's support, both emotionally and materially, our sense of benevolence would, perhaps, be both useless and purposeless. I also suggest that this quality of benevolence points us to the possibility of the sort of benevolence we would find in a being infinitely superior to ourselves, namely, God.

Whenever we find ourselves countenancing moments of crises—or, to use the expression in this book, wilderness moments—the need for a savior becomes apparent. If the wilderness moment seems to be more severe than human abilities could overcome, the need for an even more powerful Savior becomes apparent. Only a divine being, of the sort talked about in Scripture, fits this description. Not surprisingly, therefore, do we find God reminding us how we cannot live by bread alone, but by every word that proceeds from the mouth of God. Popular choruses in the praise and worship scene in Africa continue to teach this fact throughout the Christian world, one of which has gained international popularity, namely, that if God proclaims something over our lives, no one can refute him.

16

THE WILDERNESS MOMENTS OF JESUS

VERY INTERESTINGLY, JESUS found himself in a wilderness moment after getting baptized by John the Baptist. Specifically, he walked into the wilderness and fasted 40 days and nights. According to the Gospel of Mark, he was being tempted by the devil all those 40 days, including the three major temptations recorded in their entirety by the Gospel of Matthew and of Luke. In one of those temptations, Jesus quotes from Deuteronomy 8:3, underscoring the importance of depending on God under all circumstances.

The enemy, the very person responsible for Job's wilderness moments, was at it again. One of those temptations was to get Jesus to turn the rocks around him into bread in order to satisfy his hunger. Notice also how the enemy was aware that Jesus had gone for 40 days without food. Nothing seems intrinsically wrong with eating bread. To be sure, nothing seems intrinsically wrong with turning rocks into bread, assuming one could do it! However, as Newton C. Conant reminds us in his book, *Changed By Beholding Him*, turning rocks into bread in obedience to a suggestion made by the devil remains intrinsically sinful. One must not obey or follow the enemy's piece of advice, even if one is living through wilderness moments. Jesus categorically used the very passage used by Moses to remind the enemy that life is not built on material things. Life is built and founded on the very Word of God itself, which, in actuality, is the person of Jesus Christ.

What, then, did Christ imply by using this very passage? He reminded the enemy that the word of God is the source of life. In short, Jesus was claiming to be the actual source of life. In other words, Christ is the source of his own life, whether well-fed or hungry. The lack of food would not, in any way, cause him to cease to exist. Not only was he the source of his own life. Christ, also, is the source of all life. We get the reminder, from John 1:3, how through Christ all things were made and that without him nothing was made that has been made, and that in him was life, and that life was the light of all human beings.

The experience in the Judean wilderness was not the only wilderness moment Jesus experienced. Ironically, he experienced another wilderness moment in the Garden of Gethsemane. The weight of the sins of the world weighed down on him heavily. The Gospels remind us how heavy this weight was upon him in some spiritual sense that he simply fell to the ground in prayer. Your sins and my sins weighed heavily upon him. Throughout that experience, Christ prayed for relief, asking the father to spare him the agony of walking the journey to the cross—a journey Christ referred to as a "cup."

We now know how Christ suffered moments after that experience. What I wish to underscore here is an important fact: even the source of all life, namely, Christ, expressed his dependence on God the father through the exercise of prayer. He prayed his way through the wilderness of suffering, asking God for help. We get the reminder, from the Gospel of Luke, that an angel from Heaven appeared to him and strengthened him (Luke 22:43).

However, one of the most difficult wilderness moments in the life of Jesus happened at a specific moment at his crucifixion. Recall his words: "My God, my God, why have you forsaken me?"[28] This expression was an indication of God the Father's withdrawal of support for his Son. Carrying the sins of the world was bad enough. Losing the support of his Father was infinitely worse, and he felt the emptiness that followed from that very moment. Moments after that question, Christ gave a loud cry and breathed his last. That experience of emptiness and lack of support from God the Father seemed the worst kind of pain God the Son could experience in his relationship with the Father.

Shortly after our child was born, his pediatrician advised us always to take him for his regular check-ups whenever he completed specific age milestones. The first one came on his third month. The pediatrician reminded us how, on this day, they planned to give him his first four shots to keep specific

---

28 Mark 15:33

illnesses away. They called that day his "big day." He would be taken to the doctor, who would examine him, and then make specific recommendations for his shots.

When the day finally came, my wife and I knew we would have a hard time handling the experience. We decided we would tough it out and live through the experience. After all, we thought, we would not be the first parents to bring our children to the clinic for a check-up. Neither would our son be the first one to receive his shots; and surely, the nurses in the clinic were experienced in their work. For that reason, we felt, everything would be alright.

Upon arrival at the clinic, my son was his usual jovial self. He laughed heartily with the nurses. What broke my heart was how oblivious he remained concerning what was about to happen to him. He lay on the hospital table quite willingly, innocently expressing his delight at the faces smiling down at him, including mine. Even when we rested our hands on his legs, arms, and torso, he obliged.

The nurse prepared her four shots. In less than seven seconds, she gave him all four shots. I will never forget my son's facial expression when he took his first shot. It was horror, mixed with dismay, a quizzical look, and a grimace, followed by the most painful and piercing wail that ever came through his oral cavities. He felt betrayed by all these folks smiling down to him, including me. I shed a tear, but my heart was bleeding profusely. I could not look at my wife's direction. I thought about the irony of having to experience such pain in order to remain healthy.

I did wonder if both God the Father and God the Son lived through something analogous to this experience, though, of course, at an infinite level. When God the Son wondered why God the Father forsook him in this way, only a parent can understand the pain involved on the part of God the Father. God did experience that pain. Scripture reminds us that as soon as Christ gave up his spirit, the curtain of the temple was torn in two from top to bottom. Many interpretations try to explain the significance of this event. I believe they have exegetical credibility.

However, I wish to underscore an important significance of this event. When the curtain of the temple was torn in two from top to bottom, I suggest God the Father expressed his grief over the pain, suffering and death experienced by his son. God was reminding those around the crucifixion that he, too, was grieving over the loss of his son. Bear in mind how, in the Hebrew tradition, grief finds expression. Whenever individuals received the news that a loved one had died, the Hebrews passionately expressed their grief, including tearing their robes or their clothes apart.

When Jacob heard that his son, Joseph, had died, he tore his robes in grief. When Job received the news of the death of his children, he tore his robes in grief. When the chief priest heard Christ's confession claiming to be the Son of God, he tore his robes in grief, for he believed Jesus was guilty of blasphemy.

By the same motif, when God the Father heard his Son's question, and saw his Son breathe his last, he, too, tore his robes, the curtain of the temple, in two from top to bottom, as a way of expressing his grief. Still, more implications followed this gesture of tearing the curtain in two. Quite possibly,

Caiaphas the High Priest was at the temple offering sacrifices during the Passover celebrations. He must have been there when the curtain of the temple was torn in two. God seemed to be telling Caiaphas: "You tore your robe denying that Jesus is my Son. I am tearing my robes confirming to you that Jesus is my Son. He has died, and I am grieving." Perhaps that fact explains why, after watching these events unfold, the Centurion was quick to note that the person they just killed was the Son of God.

The wilderness moments Christ lived through have important lessons for us. First, we must always remember how, in the midst of our wilderness moments, life stems from Christ himself. He is the source of life. When our lives ebb away, Christ the giver of life remains our strength throughout eternity. He alone can give us the strength for daily living. After all, he reminds us how without him we can do nothing.

The second lesson, of course, is the fact that his death made our salvation from the penalty, power and presence of sin possible. His wilderness moment becomes, for us, green pastures for salvation. His death becomes life for us. His suffering becomes our relief in times of our wilderness moments. Anyone who seeks to find relief from snippets of wilderness moments afflicting them regularly can trust in Christ's salvific power.

The third lesson also comes in a very relevant way, namely: Christ's relationship with the father was broken in order to heal our relationship with God the father, and our relationships with those around us. He knows the meaning of broken relationships. He knows the implications of broken relationships. He remains fully aware of these eventualities. For this reason, he continually offers himself as a solution to our broken relationship with God, as a solution to our broken relationships with our spouses, our children, our parents, our siblings, our friends, our neighbors, and our fellow citizens.

The upshot of this entire consideration for this section, of course, is that Christ is not indifferent to our sufferings. He remains deeply involved and concerned about the wilderness moments his children live through, and he wants to bring about the intended relief you and I seek and desire. To be sure, this fact seems all we need to say concerning wilderness moments. Still, a certain aspect of wilderness moments needs to be explored, and I pursue it in the next part of this book.

PART FIVE

THE DISCIPLINE

17

THE DISCIPLINE ASPECT FOR ISRAEL

ONE OTHER ASPECT of wilderness moments, an aspect that comes through in the passage from the book of Deuteronomy, is the question of discipline. The words from Scripture come through very forcefully as follows: "Know, then, in your heart that as a man disciplines his son, so the Lord your God disciplines you."[29] God took the children of Israel through the Wilderness because he had the intention of disciplining them. The discipline they received from the Lord had the purpose of shaping their character, and making them more and more a reflection of the One who called them out of the land of slavery.

As one would imagine, this kind of discipline is never pleasant. Considerable pain follows such moments. Discipline demands a stretch beyond one's comfort zone. In order to be

---

29 Deuteronomy 8:5

shaped into the kind of persons God wants us to be, pain will have to be involved. This fact follows from the reality that we are sinners already, and in order to be purged into holiness, most of what we have become accustomed to in our being as humans will have to be removed.

What I have become in life—and I still have not arrived at the desired level of spiritual maturity—stems from moments of physical and emotional pain, some of them quite mild and some of them considerably intense. Ranging from those times I found myself under the wrath of my parents' punitive measures to the times life itself meted its own version of pain, I have been shaped into the person I am today.

On one occasion, I remember, I had to be under my parents' discipline when I sneaked out of our home. My parents had specifically asked me not to leave the home unsupervised for any reason. In defiance of this rule, I still went ahead and left the house. I had developed childhood friends in the neighborhood, and I longed to go out and play with them. Playing hide-and-seek or soccer or "thief-and-police" seemed more fun than sitting in the house trying to do my math homework. So I sneaked out. I did not do a very good job trying to hide from my parents' scrutinizing search. They seemed to have guessed exactly where I would be, and sure enough they found me. I will not venture to narrate the details of what followed this kind of disobedience. All I will venture to say is this: Three days later, sitting on a couch was painful!

One thing I could not understand was why my parents would not let me go out and play or do something fun. Clearly they had my best interests at heart. Knowing how vulnerable to mischief I would become when in the company of unsupervised boys, they wanted to spare me the consequences that would follow those boys' mischiefs. I did not understand how serious this would be until I sneaked out again one evening to play with them. As we played soccer near the house, I kicked the ball right into a glass window. The ball shattered the glass, and landed inside the dining room of our home. My mother had gone out of town. When she returned, I gathered all the courage to inform her about the event. This time round I received no punishment. What I got was a long stern lecture about following instructions and obeying my parents.

The lessons in life turned out a little more severe—from having to watch my father bury my little brother in the absence of any officiating minister, to the point at which I personally buried my father. I knew his death would only be a matter of time. I watched his health deteriorate. I did not think I could handle the news about his death. I remember praying fervently, asking the Lord to spare his life and give us many more years with him. It was not to be.

I was, at that time, a junior in Bible school. I had been sent for my internship at AIC Jericho. That experience would be my first encounter with the wonderful people I have since known in that church, and it happens to be the place I would eventually meet my spouse. While still relatively new at AIC Jericho, I remember the afternoon quite well. I had traveled to the city of Nairobi by public means to post some mail. As I walked out of the post office, I met a certain lady from my home village standing by Ronald Ngala Road, waiting for somebody to pick her up.

When she saw me, she seemed concerned. After exchanging our greetings, she asked me if I had heard from home yet. I told her I had not, and was hoping to hear from my folks. We had no cell phones in those days. Regular instant communication was difficult. However, the lady informed me how she knew my father had been admitted to a nearby hospital, and that he was feeling somewhat better.

The piece of news did not settle well with me. I went back to AIC Jericho a tired man in extremely low spirits. I then walked to our residence, which happened to be our senior pastor's house. Upon sharing what troubled me, my senior pastor immediately made arrangements for my travel. He helped me buy my bus ticket. I traveled upcountry that very night. Shortly before the bus came to a stop near my home, my uncle spotted me. I had not seen him. However, what I heard next sent chills down my spine. He called out my name and half-commandingly and half-urgently, asked me to get off the bus. He took my brief case and started walking me home. I knew at once my father was no longer with us.

I walked all the way home and found a crowd of people, all of them uncharacteristic of my people, clustered in groups and talking in low tones. Ordinarily, they would be wailing at the top of their lungs. Quite surprisingly, a deep sense of peace overtook me. I got some unexplainable strength and courage I never knew about. I suspected someone was praying for me, and possibly, quite furiously.

More importantly, God gave me the strength to stand firm during the entire preparations for the funeral. After sending word back to the authorities in AIC Jericho and to

Scott College, I stood with my mother, who, also, seemed quite strong at that time. We buried my father one week later. I preached during his funeral. Many souls gave their lives to Christ, including an alcohol vendor who supplied alcohol to the community. After this man's salvation, he stopped selling alcohol in that neighborhood, which ran in short supply for the next three weeks. He felt directly responsible for alcohol addictions in that region. Many alcoholics were known to stop by his liquor store for their daily dose of alcohol, and it wrecked their families back home. The vendor felt directly responsible for this pandemic. After meeting Christ, he knew he had to stop.

Did God discipline me through this experience? I would answer in the affirmative. Nevertheless, I would be quick to mention that he was not disciplining me because I was a sinner. I would more accurately point out that his discipline simply made me stronger in the faith. The experience was surely a wilderness moment for my brothers and sisters and, of course, my mother. The next few months would be followed by days of intense grief and extreme sorrow on my mother's part. Our family seemed to fall apart after my uncles took advantage of my father's death to harass my mother. Rather than fight back, we all decided to relocate my mother to a place where she would have peace and quiet.

God used my father's death to give me the strength I needed in the face of death. He assured me how no matter what I would face, the important thing was his presence in my life. He continued to build me and to strengthen me in this journey called life. Whereas I would do anything to see my father again, I am thankful for what I have become even in his absence. Of course I wish he was around to meet my spouse and my son. Still, I always find comfort in the assurance of our final reunion, which will last forever when the Lord returns.

The nation of Israel had its share of discipline. Their discipline came, however, as a result of living a life of rebellion against God. As already noted, they built a golden calf, contrary to the commandments God had given them about not building any graven images and worshiping them. God cherished his relationship with his children and was not willing to trade that relationship with anything else. Strangely, the children of Israel, even after seeing God's hand at work in their lives, winked quite favorably toward idolatry, much to God's divine anger. This state of affairs did not settle well for them, and God used their wilderness moments to discipline them and make them more willing to turn to him as their God.

18

The Temptation to Backslide

DISCIPLINE SEEMS ENDEMIC in life. In other words, it is widespread. What we must ask, in such instances, is whether we think wilderness moments build us up or tear us down. God disciplines us in order to build us up, and we must learn the various lessons presented to us during those times. Otherwise, those times would be wasted.

Take the case of athletes, for example. They put their bodies through rigorous physical exercises. They train hard. They live through intense physical pain. They do this in order to prepare themselves for specific competitions. They subject themselves to harder training in order to ensure success when their day of competition comes.

Notice, also, how beneficial to one's health such intense physical training really becomes. Nutritionists and physicians continue to remind us of the great benefits one gets from cardiovascular exercises and from resistance training, One's cholesterol levels improve, one's heart gets stronger, and generally, one experiences good health. In short, physical training really does shape the individual, making him or her even healthier.

One person, in Scripture, who seemed to have benefited greatly from wilderness moments, was Caleb.[30] He was strong. He was fit. He was swift. Old age never got the better of him. For those 40 years in the wilderness, he became stronger and stronger. To be sure, he seemed to have benefited more from the wilderness moment than he would have been without it. Moreover, when the Israelites finally settled in the land flowing with milk and honey, Caleb's testimony of how physically fit he became stands out forcefully. The experience in the wilderness brought out the best in him, both physically and spiritually. Physically his fitness prevailed. Spiritually, his faith in God remained intact. This state of affairs first got illustrated when he went out to spy the land they were to possess. When everyone else was melting in fear, Caleb and Joshua saw opportunity. They were ready to go and take over the land. The wilderness moment did not make them lose their faith in God.

Quite possibly, we can continue to turn away from God during those wilderness moments. They have brought about states of unbelief in some cases. I have, for example, noted the case of a New Testament professor who abandoned his belief in God while countenancing this very idea. Also, one of the originators of the theory of evolution, Charles Darwin, turned away from God completely when, we are told, his daughter died. At that time, he became an agnostic, namely, one who believes

---

30 Joshua 14:6–15

God is unknowable. In other words, he came to the conclusion that one cannot know whether or not God exists. Notice how the experience of suffering brought him to this conclusion.

Ordinarily, those who turn away from God as a result of living through wilderness moments do so because they think a loving God would not allow his children to suffer. Hence, if God exists, he must not be very loving. To be sure, they would maintain, if God exists, he is rather cruel, and because a cruel God remains inconsistent with the loving God talked about in the Bible, the God talked about in the Bible does not exist.

The person advancing this kind of claim remains quite unaware of the fact that the God of the Bible really does allow pain to come our way, not because he is cruel, but because he lovingly disciplines us, using specific wilderness moments, to shape us into becoming the very persons he wants us to be. He desires in us a specific kind of spiritual formation, which can only be made possible by experiencing a wilderness moment.

We find evidence of this kind explicated in various parts of Scripture. When Paul, for example, lived through a wilderness moment, God had a specific message for him. God reminded him that he had to be weak in order to be strong. Even more importantly, Paul introduces the wilderness moment by noting that it came for the purpose of keeping him from becoming conceited and boastful.[31] Paul had received numerous revelations from God, and Paul himself seemed to be aware of how those kinds of revelations would, eventually, make him proud. To keep this possibility of

31 2 Corinthians 12:7–10

pride from becoming a fact, God sent a messenger of the enemy to buffet him, to beat him again and again. It was a moment of discipline he had to live through in order to be shaped and become the kind of person God wanted him to be. The result, in Paul's life, turned out quite dramatic. Paul realized how strong he could be even when he was weak.

When God allows us to live through wilderness moments, we might need to ask ourselves how we think he is trying to shape us, and what areas in our lives we think God is trying to correct. Sometimes a quick reflection on our part will help reveal the answer to this question. At other times such a revelation might take an entire lifetime. By noting this fact, I simply admit that we have no specific formula of figuring out what kinds of lessons we would have to learn. Each lesson seems unique to each experience. This reality of the uniqueness of each lesson leads me, therefore, to suggest what, I think, seems the only logical resolve, namely, to sit and try to figure out what, exactly, the Lord might be trying to communicate in a given situation. Quite possibly, God might desire to get a person's attention by letting the person live through those moments in the wilderness, and the best way to do so would be to let the person experience that very moment.

The worst a person can do, at such times, is to turn away from God. When one turns away from God, we must ask, after the manner of paradoxical writer G. K. Chesterton, what then, does the person turn to? To turn away from God implies one must turn to something less than God—possibly another human being, or something worse. When this happens, wilderness moments begin to get meaningless. Falling into a state of meaninglessness during such moments brings about a crisis of existence. One begins to wonder why one exists at all. Usually, those who turn away from God in such times, and then experience a statement of resultant meaninglessness, begin to get suicidal.

This fact came across as a warning from the Algerian philosopher, Albert Camus. He warned us of how suicide becomes a very live option to individuals who find life meaningless, whether from pain or from another source. This fact comes across to us as a sad reality.

You and I need not live through this experience. We might need to take some time out of our busy schedule, a schedule we try to observe because of an attempt on our part to overcome specific wilderness moments, and in the process use those times of reflection to figure out how we think God might be trying to shape us. This kind of resolution might be one that every believer, at some point in his or her life, will have to take if we wish to figure out what sorts of things God might be trying to accomplish in our lives. If one lives through those moments without coming to understand the purpose God is trying to fulfill in one's life, then the experience becomes a wasted opportunity, such as the opportunity experienced by Miriam and Aaron who, while in the wilderness, made fun of Moses' Cushitic wife.[32] This moment need not be wasted. It stands to yield meaningful fruits as a product shaped by God's molding hand, and that product, I dare say, could be you.

---

32 Numbers 12

19

THE PRESENCE OF GOD

ONE OF THE difficulties humans routinely face in the advent of wilderness moments involves the apparent loneliness that follows. The amazing thing about wilderness moments, for the Christian, involves the fact that he or she is never alone. Of course, humanly speaking, friends may abandon the person living through that experience. A friend of mine, for example, spoke of how his brother got incarcerated, and while in jail never received even a single visit from his own pastor. In a very real sense, this friend felt quite lonely while living through a wilderness moment.

In many ways individuals feel a sense of loneliness when countenancing those moments. They express their feeling of walking through that journey, all by themselves, without someone to walk along with them. They struggle with the terror of loneliness. It afflicts them like a disease, and no one seems present to provide a helping hand.

However, from a spiritual perspective, God is ever present to the person struggling through those moments. Notice how God's presence remained abundantly clear when the Israelites wandered through the Wilderness. For example, Deuteronomy 8:2 indicates how the Lord led the children of Israel those 40 years in the wilderness. He was there with them, testing them in order to reveal what was in their hearts, whether or not they would keep his commandments. He did not let them walk through the wilderness all by themselves.

Notice also, that in the process of testing them, he also humbled them by feeding them with manna. He would not have fed them if he remained distant from them while they wandered in the desert. This fact can only mean he was there with them throughout their time there. Besides that miraculous provision for their food, God used the experience to teach them to depend on him. He would not have made them depend on him if he remained distant from them. In order to have them depend on him, somehow they would have needed to know he was near them. Fourth, if he needed to discipline them, then, somehow, his closeness, or his nearness would be necessary, and because we know, from verse 5, how God disciplines his children in a manner analogous to parents disciplining their children, God would need to be close to those very children.

In other words, while God took the Israelites through the wilderness, he did not leave them alone. He walked with them every step of the way, year after year, decade after decade. They saw him perform miraculous signs before their very eyes. They saw him punish wayward Israelites who rejected his leadership. They saw him communicate with Moses in a certain sense. In all these experiences, the wilderness moments of the Israelites happened when God was closest to them.

We find a similar experience in the life of Job. Shortly after Job lived through his own version of the wilderness, God seemed distant. Several times, Job wondered when God would show up. He pleaded with God to show up in order for him to present his case to God. After false counsel based on a false interpretation of Job's experience, God did finally show up. Moreover, God asked Job more than 65 questions, and the nature of his questions suggested a full awareness of the conversation taking place between Job and his three friends. God reprimanded the friends for their failure to interpret Job's situation correctly. All these facts illustrate how God was not really that far from Job in the first place.

All these serve to underscore the important lesson that God never leaves his suffering children alone. When they live through moments of pain and suffering, he walks through those experiences with them. Sometimes he chooses to take those pains and suffering out of the lives of his children and end them completely. At other times, some thinkers have noted correctly that God decides to allow the storms to rage on in the wilderness, and, instead, chooses to calm the hearts of his children by comforting them, and assuring them of his goodness and mercy.

Wilderness moments remain, truly quite troubling when seen in and of themselves. No one wants to live through them. However, when we know that God can enable us to live through those moments victoriously through his presence in our lives during those times, and beyond, we can rest assured he will walk with us through each step, and allow us to overcome those moments with resounding victory.

You are never alone. God never intended for you to be alone. Even when you seemingly feel as if you are alone, find comfort in the realization that God wishes to walk this difficult journey with you. Needless to say, questions still remain, questions whose answers remain unavailable this side of Heaven, until you and I land on the other side of Heaven, a side poets call "the blissful shore."

So why choose to believe in God in the midst of unanswered questions? The reason, I think, though not very simple, seems very credible and, I think, can be formulated as follows: The opposite of choosing to believe in God is choosing not to believe in God. A state of unbelief, then, becomes our answer to those wilderness moments. This state of unbelief does, indeed, come with inadequate human answers. Moreover, those answers remain brutal. I do not recommend this state at all.

First of all, the answers involve the belief that God does not exist, and for this reason, we must face a world of suffering without God. In other words, we must face the brutalities of this world all by ourselves, and that reality remains a brute fact. If our world is truly a godless world, wherein God does not exist, this must be the conclusion we will face. Our pain and suffering will forever remain purposeless and meaningless. No one, for example, will be required to pay or held accountable for inflicting our bodies with deadly diseases such as cancer. No one will be held accountable for inflicting this world with tsunamis, earthquakes and hurricanes that have, killed hundreds of thousands of people. No one will be called to pay for influencing human minds to rape innocent girls and children. To be sure, both rapists and saints will all end up in the same place, namely, in a state of nonexistence. In such a world, Adolf Hitler, Idi Amin, Mother Teresa, Billy Graham and the Apostle Paul will all end up in the same place. Such a world, surely, defies our sense of morality and justice. Why would such a world endow humans with a sense of justice only for that very world to deceive us that an overall sense of justice remains extinct, thereby leaving un-dealt with all instances of injustice?

A world of the sort described by the Bible, however, presents a radically different picture. In such a world, the enemy bringing about tsunamis, hurricanes and earthquakes will be held accountable for killing hundreds of thousands of innocent people. In such a world, the enemy will have to be held accountable for influencing and tempting morally bankrupt individuals to rape innocent girls and children. Such a world assures us of how good actions will be rewarded and bad actions will be punished. It assures us that evil people who committed mass murders, if they died without repentance, will truly be held accountable, and will be required to pay, with their own lives forever, for the pain they inflicted on humanity. The Biblical world has endowed humans with a sense of justice, and it assures us that an overall sense of justice exists in such a way that all immoral acts will be punished.

In such a world, God is presented as remaining ever-present among his people, even when he does not seem to act, as was the case for Job. Simply because he does not seem to act does not mean he is not acting at all. God might still be working and acting behind the scenes in order to bring about a more comprehensive form of redemption and deliverance for his people.

I present this very idea of God's presence to you, not only because it remains underscored throughout the Bible, but also because you, the believer, needs, as I do, a constant and frequent reminder of how God walks with his children through their suffering and pain. This fact has remained trustworthy from the Old Testament times through the New Testament times. Christ underscores this fact even when he issued The Great Commission. To be sure, interesting stories illustrating this fact remain prevalent even in our culture today.

One that comes to mind, and often quoted by believers, involves a person who dreamed he had a conversation with God, wherein God showed him two sets of footprints. God seemed to be reviewing the believer's life for the believer while he walked through his life's journey. As they viewed the set of prints, God informed the believer, that the first set belonged to God, and the other set belonged to the believer. As they followed along on those sets of footprints, they got to a point where the second set was no longer visible. Upon inquiry, God informed the believer why there was only one set. God told the believer how the set reduced to one whenever the believer encountered difficulties. This realization troubled the believer. He wondered why God would let him walk through the difficult journey alone, without God's help. God, as most people familiar with the story remember, reminded the believer that he really was not alone. Rather, he was carrying the believer on his back during those moments of suffering and trials.

The fact that God walks with us through our wilderness moments should remain forever assuring for all of us. It is a fact whose truth we must always cherish. Knowing this fact helps to make the difference between walking through our wilderness moments successfully and failing when those moments come our way. You and I have the privilege of encouraging the unbelieving world that such moments need not drive them away from God. If anything, God's presence can still be felt even when accosted by such moments. When they come our way, we can find assurance and comfort that God will show us how to walk through the journey, in much the same way he let the children of Israel walk through theirs.

20

THE TRIUMPH

A REMARKABLE LINE MOSES gives in Deuteronomy 8:4 runs as follows: "Your clothes did not wear out and your feet did not swell these 40 years." This line comes immediately after Moses points out to the Israelites the importance of depending on God. He reminded them of God's victorious sustenance in their lives through those 40 years. They were first-hand witnesses of how God came through for them. God preserved their wardrobes, so to speak, without a single malfunction countenanced by any one of them!

I look at my own life and the story remains radically different. I notice, for example, how I need to get new clothes very often. I cannot count the number of clothes I have gone through for the past five years! In none of those times did I live through experiences of the sort Moses is describing. My clothes wear out quite fast, needing to be replaced with new clothes regularly when compared and contrasted to the state of affairs countenanced by the Israelites, and I need not mention the situation with my five-year old son, who outgrows his clothes uncomfortably fast. Any parent would know how this state of affairs plays itself out in such young lives.

Turning to the Israelites we find a radically different story. Their clothes remained intact. None of them needed a change of clothes even when the harshest desert conditions confronted them on a daily basis in the wilderness. God was underscoring to them the importance of trusting and depending on him as they walked through this difficult journey. The testimony of their victorious walk through the wilderness stood right before their eyes, and they could not deny it. They saw how God sustained their lives with food and sustained their wardrobes with clothes.

Not only did their clothes remain intact. Their feet did not swell either. In other words, God preserved their feet, sustaining them with agility. God kept them healthy and strong all the way. One would have expected them to live through excruciations that came along with such situations. Those excruciations did not materialize in any tangible way. In short, God kept them healthy from the time they left Egypt to the time they reached the Promised Land. Anyone looking for a Biblical example of God leading his children to paths where his grace necessarily keeps them will immediately note that the Israelite journey through the wilderness is certainly one of them.

How, then, should one live a life that prevails against one's wilderness moments? I suggest several possible things one must do. First of all, one must remind oneself of God's presence through constant prayer. Certain testimonies concerning the evangelist Billy Graham portray him as a deeply prayerful man. When asked what he considers to be the three most important things in a believer's life, his answer was simple: the first one was prayer, the second one was prayer and the third one was prayer. For Billy Graham, prayer was indispensable to the Christian life. Before making important decisions in ministry, Christ would spend a whole night in prayer. When he got busy, he prayed. When he experienced his wilderness moments, he was fasting. I also assume he was praying. He did pray in the Garden of Gethsemane, and that allowed him to have the power to overcome the kinds of tests, trials and temptations brought about by wilderness moments. Recall how Christ himself prescribed this activity of prayer in his piece of advice to the disciples when he said, "Pray that you may not enter into temptation."

Prayer gives you the fuel that drives you through the wilderness. Christ used it successfully, and I think you too can employ this very important discipline in your life. Many Christians continue to testify about the value of prayer in their lives. Not only do they find, in prayer, the means by which they find help in times of need. They also find, in prayer, the means by which God's presence remains a reality for them. I have seen God do powerful things in my life through prayer, none of which could have been accomplished by my own abilities alone. These works from God continue to remind me of his presence in my life, which is more important, by far, than merely trying to use God as a slot machine.

The second thing one must do to prevail against one's wilderness moments is to listen to the voice of God by abiding constantly in his word. When Christ was in the wilderness, not only did he pray, he depended on the very word of God to grant him victory, the very word, which Moses used when he reminded us of how our very lives depended on it. Dwelling in God's word, according to the Bible, surely provides one with the arsenal for conquering the wilderness moments one experiences. Notice how the enemy got vanquished with the word whenever Christ quoted it against him at each stage of the temptation. Paul does not call this word "the Sword of the Spirit" by accident. Not only does the word begin to get useful when used against the enemy during wilderness moments that come from him, the word is also useful in sustaining the believer through wilderness moments used by God to help the believer mature in him. In this way, the believer remains constantly reminded of God's presence even when the temptation to doubt his presence rages on.

I routinely memorize huge portions of Scripture as one of the ways to dwell in God's word. This exercise proves invaluable in empowering me to overcome temptations that would, otherwise, have vanquished me. The psalmist was right by noting that hiding God's word in one's heart keeps one from sinning against God. I can vouch for the fact that the activity truly does work. I have been on both ends: succumbing to temptations and overcoming them. The former happened when I distanced myself from God's word. The latter became a reality as I took the time to meditate and memorize Scripture. The more I bathed my mind with God's word, the more I experienced the joy of victory.

The third thing a believer struggling through wilderness moments ought to do to prevail throughout these moments is to fellowship with other believers going through these moments. Those who have experienced such moments and have come through them victoriously also become very useful allies, as we read in the words of the apostle Paul. He writes: "Praise be to God and Father of our Lord Jesus Christ, the Father of compassion and the God of all comfort, who comforts us in all our troubles, so that we can comfort those in any trouble with the comfort we ourselves have received from God."[33] Fellow believers who prevail against wilderness moments victoriously, with remarkable understanding of their situations, often find themselves capable of helping those walking through that journey. Only a person who knows what losing a son means will stand with the individual struggling through similar moments.

The fourth thing one could do is to live each day at a time, knowing how, in Christ, we have the promise of a final victory against the moment. This attitude is an attitude of hope. One must live meaningfully in the present inspired by the hope of a future redemption. The down side to this kind of thinking is how one remains unsure of when such victory will come. However, the up side to this kind of thinking is that Scripture does present us with the assurance of living victoriously through our wilderness moments. The question is not whether or not wilderness moments will ever come. Such moments remain guaranteed in life. The question, therefore, is how we plan to live through those moments when they come. Christian believers continue to find assurance that when

---

33 2 Corinthians 1:3-4

such moments come, they need not conquer the believer. The believer will rise above them with the assurance of victory in the final analysis. Such hope cannot be found in any academic disciplines available in our universities. Such disciplines only succeed in reminding us how the universe is slowly losing its energy, and, someday, will end catastrophically.

The Christian view underscores the very fact of a final victory of life over death, of good over evil, of joy over pain, and, of course, of God over the enemy. No other discipline, I claim, can give us such hope with the finality of this sort. Only God can, and this claim is true because such disciplines are the works of human minds. The hope is the guarantee from the very throne of God himself. My prayer, then, is for you, the reader, to prevail against your wilderness moments through the assurance we find in the death, resurrection and return of Christ.

Appendix

U NLESS ONE REALLY wants to pursue the issues addressed in this section, namely, the problem of evil, I warn you, the reader, that this section tends to get quite heavy in terms of the materials presented. As already noted, the theme of this work falls under a broader theme dominating current debates in philosophy of religion ordinarily referred to as the problem of evil. The problem routinely finds its nuance in the contention that Christians lack the right to believe in the existence of an omnipotent and omnibenevolent God if they fail to reconcile that belief with the facts and reality of evil, evil being understood in this context as pain and suffering.

Moreover, philosophers normally distinguish between moral evil and natural evil. Moral evil, we are informed, seems to include flawed character traits of human beings and instances of pain and suffering resulting from those flawed character traits. Natural evil includes instances of pain and suffering brought about by processes of nature such as terminal illnesses, earthquakes, tsunamis, tornadoes, landslides, and similar instances.

Contemporary philosophers of religion provide useful categories of this problem as a way of highlighting the various ways in which we can understand its forcefulness. Since the terrain remains quite vast, I need not explicate each version of the problem here. What I hope to do is to highlight two of the most famous ones and give a brief explication of what both entail.

Take, for example, the first category, often referred to as the logical problem of evil. Briefly stated, the logical version of the problem of evil contends how belief in the existence of God remains logically incompatible with the facts and reality of evil. The version challenges the Christian believer to show how this apparent logical contradiction could get diffused.

J. L. Mackie seems to be one of the most famous raisers of this objection. He formulated his objection by drawing attention to three specific claims accepted by Christian theologians, namely: God is all good, God is all powerful, and evil exists. According to Mackie, these three claims seem contradictory. If one accepts any two of them, the third one will yield a contradiction. However, Mackie immediately adds that this contradiction may not be readily apparent. To be sure, we must add a fourth and a fifth claim, also accepted by Christian theologians, in order for us to appreciate the nature of the contradiction.

Exactly what claims does Mackie have in mind? The two claims, Mackie suggests, run as follows: A good being will want to eliminate evil as far as it can, and we should find no limits to what an all-powerful being could do. These two claims seem true of God. Therefore, combining them with the first two of the original three statements yields the conclusion that evil does not exist. This resultant conclusion contradicts one of the claims that evil exists, a claim accepted by Christian theology. Thus, Mackie would argue how the postulates of Christian theology would lead the Christian thinker to conclude both that evil exists and evil does not exist. For this reason, Mackie concludes that Christianity remains positively irrational.

Christian philosopher Alvin Plantinga famously refuted Mackie's charge by showing the innocuous nature of the charge itself. Let me highlight two of the several ways in which Plantinga demonstrated the weakness of Mackie's charge. Plantinga tries to show how, in order for Mackie's objection to succeed, Mackie's additional claims must be a necessary truth namely: a good being will want to eliminate evil as far as it possibly can. A necessary truth is one that cannot be false under any conditions. Plantinga cites various ways in which a claim of the sort Mackie alludes to could be false. He cites examples wherein one could imagine how someone who, by all accounts, is good and wants to eliminate evil as far as he or she can, but somehow fails. Plantinga explores possible ways in which this state of affairs can play itself out. Trying to capture the crux of Plantinga's argument in this section would, perhaps, takes us too far afield, and quite possibly beyond where you, the reader, might be willing to go.

However, I believe an important piece of Plantinga's rebuttal to Mackie merits attention. In order to show that even in a world where the facts and reality of evil confront us God can still be understood to exist, Plantinga appeals to what he calls *The Free Will Defense*. Herein, Plantinga notes how a world with significantly free creatures remains more valuable than a world without any free creatures at all. Even though God can create free creatures, he cannot determine those creatures to do the right thing all the time specifically because he would be preempting their freedom if he did. Therefore, for freedom to make any sense at all, God cannot create free creatures capable of moral good without, as a result, creating them to be capable of moral evil. God's elimination of the possibility of moral evil entails eliminating the possibility of moral good. However, Plantinga notes the sad reality that some creatures did go wrong in the exercise of their freedom, and that explains why evil exists today in a world created by God. This fact, though, does not undercut God's goodness. Neither does it undercut his omnipotence.

Plantinga's Free Will Defense seems widely regarded by a wide variety of philosophers on both sides of the debate (namely, both theists and atheists) as a successful objection to J. L. Mackie. To be sure, even Mackie himself acknowledged the rebuttal's success. Some remain unconvinced. Their skepticisms arise from their observation that Plantinga's Free Will Defense seems an answer only to the problem of moral evil. However, they observe, the defense fails to address the problem of natural evil. To be sure, Plantinga does address the concern, though quite briefly, when he postulates how we could plausibly view evil as the result of the actions of non-human free willed agents. If Plantinga is correct, his view would imply that all evil, after all, should be regarded as moral evil.

At any rate, Plantinga's rebuttal against the charge raised by Mackie's logical problem of evil really does seem successful. With respect to other versions of the problem of evil, rebuttals have been slightly less successful—though enough, on the one hand, to sustain belief in the existence of God and, on the other to encourage further research on this field.

Consider, for example, the evidential problem of evil. Whereas many philosophers believe J. L. Mackie systematized the logical version of the problem of evil, the formulation of the evidential version of the problem of evil does not belong to any specific philosopher. Stated quite generally, the evidential version of the problem of evil contends that the facts and reality of evil in the world today provide evidence for the non-existence of God. A variant of this version, described by Christian philosopher Michael L. Peterson as the probabilistic problem of evil, finds the existence of God improbable (50 percent or less) given the facts and reality of evil.

We find more pointed versions from two atheists, William Rowe and Michael Martin. For example, according to William Rowe, no *good* we know of is of the sort that justifies God to permit horrific cases of suffering such as the rape and murder of a five-year-old girl or the painful death of a fawn in a forest fire. Therefore, we find no good all that justifies God in permitting these kinds of evils. For this reason, God does not exist. To be sure, only an actual good could be of the sort that allows God to permit horrific cases of suffering. However, we know of no actual good of this kind.

This charge from William Rowe seems to find expression in another different version of the problem of evil called the problem of gratuitous evil. Other philosophers have termed this version as the problem of innocent suffering. The problem seeks to know why God, if he exists, lets his innocent children suffer. One will recall how the book of Job seems hinged on this very motif. Stronger versions find expression from more militant atheists who find themselves charging God with wrongdoing (a gesture declared sinful in Job 1:22). Usually, such charges contend that God remains morally at fault for allowing innocent people to suffer.

Michael Martin approaches the problem from a different angle. He notes how theists uphold God's omnipotence. If God is, indeed, omnipotent, Martin argues, he would prevent evil unless such evil were logically necessary. However, such evil is not logically necessary and, for that reason, God is not omnipotent. Similarly, Martin notes how theists uphold God's omnibenevolence. If God were, indeed, omnibenevolent, Martin argues again, then God would prevent evil unless he had sufficient reasons to allow such evils to exist in great abundance. However, Martin continues, we find no sufficient reasons for God to allow evil in great abundance, and for this reason, God is not all good. Therefore, because God is neither good nor powerful and evil exists, these conclusions seem to be evidence against the existence of an omnibenevolent and omnipotent God.

To respond to this charge, Alvin Plantinga, William Alston and Stephen Wyskstra draw our attention to the following possibilities: Suppose God has a reason for permitting horrific cases of suffering to occur (such as those already mentioned), and suppose we try to figure out what that reason might be. Coming up with the right answer would seem unlikely. We should not be surprised that God's reasons for some of what he does or allows will completely escape us, on the one hand, in light of the fact that God himself remains eternally omniscient while our cognitive faculties, on the other hand, remains limited. Job found himself face to face with this reality. Even after God answered Job from the heavens, Job still could not understand God's answers.

Given the general success of the response Christian theists have offered, from a philosophical perspective, in their response to the skepticism raised by the problem of evil, belief in the existence of God from a philosophical perspective remains a very viable option. As noted by world famous apologist Ravi Zacharias, when skeptics often try to advance the belief that God is dead, God always outlives his pallbearers. The very fact that belief in God continues to dominate worldviews, especially in the Global South, should furnish us with this hint, namely, that he is, indeed, alive. Only those who have experienced him know this truth well. If you have experienced him in your life, you know the joy I discuss in these pages. If you have not experienced him, giving God a chance in your life is only fair.

Author Information

J OSEPH B. ONYANGO Okello holds a Bachelor of Theology
Degree from Scott Theological College, a Master of Divinity
and a Master of Arts in Church Music, both from Asbury
Theological Seminary, A Master of Arts in Philosophy and
a PhD in Philosophy, both from the University of Kentucky.
He has authored several books, including *"Revisiting God,"*
"Evil and Pain" and *"Heaven: God's Solution to Human Pain."*
Currently, Joseph teaches Philosophy and Christian Ethics at
Asbury Theological Seminary's Dunnam Campus in Florida,
USA, where he lives with his wife, Sophie, and their son
Sean. He is also an assistant pastor at First United Methodist
Church, Oviedo, Florida.

Made in the USA
Charleston, SC
12 July 2016